D1189570

CITY MANAGERS
AND
SCHOOL SUPERINTENDENTS

CITY MANAGERS
AND
SCHOOL SUPERINTENDENTS

Response to Community Conflict

Harmon Zeigler,
Ellen Kehoe,
and Jane Reisman

PRAEGER SPECIAL STUDIES • PRAEGER SCIENTIFIC

New York • Philadelphia • Eastbourne, UK
Toronto • Hong Kong • Tokyo • Sydney

Library of Congress Cataloging in Publication Data

Zeigler, L. Harmon (Luther Harmon), 1936–
  City managers and school superintendents.

  Bibliography: p.
  Includes index.
  1. School superintendents and principals—United
States—Case studies. 2. City managers—United States—
Case studies. 3. School districts—United States—
Administration—Case studies. 4. Conflict management—
United States—Case studies. I. Kehoe, Ellen.
II. Reisman, Jane. III. Title.
LB2831.72.Z44 1985   379.1′535   84-15973
ISBN 0-03-001408-5 (alk. paper)

Published and Distributed by the
Praeger Publishers Division
(ISBN Prefix 0-275)
of Greenwood Press, Inc.,
Westport, Connecticut

Published in 1985 by Praeger Publishers
CBS Educational and Professional Publishing,
a Division of CBS Inc.
521 Fifth Avenue, New York, NY 10175 USA

56789 052 987654321

Printed in the United States of America
on acid-free paper

Contents

Acknowledgments

The initial idea that ultimately became this book was suggested to the senior author by Harvey Tucker, then at the University of Oregon, as a logical extension of previous work. Together we developed the basic theories that guided the project. While I was living out of the country, Harvey kept the project going. Harvey left in 1979. His place was taken by Jack Polito, Jane Reisman, and Ken Rocco. These three worked up the interview schedules and questionnaires. Rocco left the project and was replaced by Ellen Kehoe. The usual attrition meant that Kehoe and Reisman were at Oregon during the final data analysis. These authors, listed alphabetically, brought different perspectives to the book, making it a genuinely collaborative project. Reisman, a sociologist, expanded my original notions of professionalism to include the function of professionalism in public bureaucracies; Kehoe, from educational administration, provided a check on my tendency to view the world from the point of view of normative theories of democracy.

Among those at Oregon who were of unusual help, Bob Mattson and Jane Arends clearly should be singled out. Bob saw his primary role as that of insulating us from meddlesome bureaucracies, while Jane translated our prose into the arcane jargon of federal grant monitors (I was pleased to learn that we did indeed yield "deliverables," "milestones," and "products" while all the while I thought we were writing a book). The numerous drafts, reports, and the like were typed with skill by Dorothy Van Cleef. The final draft was typed by Terry Williams. Wynn DeBevoise edited our manuscripts with skill and patience.

Our sincere thanks are extended to those city managers and school superintendents who participated in the various phases of the project. With rare exception they were generous with their time and candid in their responses.

Finally, we thank Dorothy Breitbart of Praeger for her judgment.

Harmon Zeigler

List of Tables

List of Charts

Introduction: Background of the Study

This book is about city managers and superintendents, a comparison that may appear odd, especially to educationists accustomed to years of political and institutional isolation. It is, however, a compellingly logical mode of inquiry.

The conclusions reached here are the result of many years' study of the responsiveness of school administrators to the public and most recently, a three-year research project funded by the National Institute of Education through the Center for Educational Policy and Management at the University of Oregon to compare the conflict management behavior of school superintendents and city managers.

Two sets of assumptions have guided our study. First, we believe it appropriate to begin with studies of conflict management in the primary governmental units of American education—school districts. We have left the task of studying conflict management within and among the federal, state, and individual school or classroom levels to others or to subsequent studies. There is, we believe, a great deal that can be learned about the management of conflict that occurs at the level of the school district.

Second, we assume that systematic studies of conflict management in school districts should be comparative. We think that the most useful research for superintendents will allow them to draw upon both the experiences of their peers in other districts and the experiences of city managers, their counterparts in city governments. Both the governance structures of school districts and cities were subjected to similar reforms intended to bring depoliticization and to render them more technological. But there have been few research studies to suggest the degree to which comparable pre-reform structures retained their similarities after being subjected to reform. We think it worthwhile to consider the degree to which the allegedly beleaguered nature of the superintendency is really different from that of others similarly situated.

Much of the discussion and analysis in this book is based upon interviews with superintendents and city managers located in two major metropolitan areas: San Francisco and Chicago. These two areas were selected by means of a stratified probability sample. A list of Standard Metropolitan Statistical Areas was examined in order to determine which areas had the highest concentration of city managers and superintendents in contiguous locations. All school districts have superintendents, but city managers are more often found in the West and in suburbs. Of six metropolitan areas having a high concentration of city managers and superintendents, Chicago and San Francisco were selected because, taken together, they offered a rich diversity of socioeconomic conditions not found in the other cities. A target population of approximately 100, drawn equally from both groups, was developed using a chart of random numbers. Our final sample consisted of 104 people, about equally divided between city managers and superintendents.

These executives were interviewed in person by the authors of this book. The interview schedule was developed in a series of pretests beginning in Oregon and culminating in Los Angeles, with substantial revisions between each wave. The interviews were conducted during the winter of 1980–81, and ranged in length from 45 minutes to two hours. Additionally, mail questionnaires of a routine nature, which had been mailed previously, were collected at the time of the interview. While in the various sites, legal, economic, and political information, generally available from minutes of meetings and other public records, was also obtained.

Much of the variable construction is apparent. Two measures, which are used routinely in the study, deserve a brief explanation. Professionalism is measured by a modified version of Richard Hall's Professional Attitude Scale. The modification was undertaken in order to make it more compatible with the expectations of public administrators. For instance, questions concerning complete work autonomy were minimized while questions concerning perception of the importance of work, self-regulation, reference to professional peers, and the importance of professional organizations were enhanced. The revised test proved reliable at .62, well within the conventionally accepted limits of reliability.

The Professionalism Scale is reproduced in Appendix A. Each response was ranked from 1 to 5, and each respondent given a mean score. However, much of the analysis is based upon the use of dichotomous rather than continuous data.

Leadership, the other routinely used index, was developed during the course of the five waves of pretesting. The items address executives' initiative in advocating policy changes, the degree to which they take stands on controversial issues, and their activity in legislative elections (see Appendix B). This scale also met the conventional tests for reliability. Responses were ranked from 1 to 4, and mean scores assigned to each respondent, but again we elected to use dichotomous variables. We did this for a variety of reasons. Most important, many of the significant independent variables—conflict management behavior for example—could only be measured in a nominal way. Thus we treated all variables as nonparametric, admittedly a deviation from the more accepted practice of pushing variables up to interval data. There is of course information loss. In our case, there appeared to be no significant information loss or distortion, as the correlations between the two forms of the same variables were significant. Thus we present our data in traditional contingency table analysis. However, in more technical reports we relied equally upon log-linear analysis (Reisman 1982), a technique which allows the examination of several nominally measured variables simultaneously. The tabular material presented in this book also passed the more rigorous, but tedious, test.

This book is the final portion of a trilogy begun in 1974 with *Governing American Schools* and continuing in 1980 with *Professionals vs the Public*. Those familiar with these earlier books will recognize a different emphasis. While the first books in the trilogy were heavily data reliant, this one is more argumentative: the data are used in conjunction with a variety of other sources to make the comparative argument more appealing. More than a decade of research has thus come to a halt. Many of the conclusions and arguments of the previous research are strengthened, and others are modified, but the thrust of the research has not changed. Government is a contest between experts and lay persons. The tension is unavoidable, and its resolution does not rest with yet more rational technologies of conflict management but rather with common sense.

CITY MANAGERS
AND
SCHOOL SUPERINTENDENTS

—1—

Professionalism and Responsiveness

The Belief in Expertise

Although their differences are substantial, superintendents and city managers have one essential characteristic in common: they are professionally trained experts held accountable to lay legislatures. The institutions and rules that govern this accountability are similar for both are products of the urban reform movement of the late nineteenth and early twentieth centuries. Professionally trained administrators are employed by lay boards of education or city councils, usually elected by nonpartisan, at-large ballots. These lay legislators are, of course, faithful to the tradition of American grass roots democracy, but they may well be no match for their more skilled yet legally subordinate employees, managers, and superintendents. This inherent tension between professionalism and responsiveness is a dilemma for public servants, and indeed for democracies. It is a dilemma that, although presumably subject to solution, has yet to be resolved.

Traditional democratic theory holds that political influence ought to follow lines of legal authority. Administrators in school districts and city governments should follow the instructions of their constituents (the public). Boards of education and city councils appoint superintendents and city managers and may remove them when they so desire. Superintendents and city managers are administrative officers responsive to legislatures which, in turn, are accountable to the public.

1

Models do not describe reality, however, and we would be foolish to suggest that a facile method of resolving tension between experts and lay persons is an easily followed pattern. Theoretically, it is. The function of legislatures is to represent. Their only source of political influence rests on the claim to be representatives of the public will. If they are not responsive, as is frequently the case, at least there is a standard by which they can be measured. No more damning charge can be leveled against an elected official than the one of being "nonresponsive." No matter how decisions are made, Americans believe that the content of political decisions should not be at variance with public sentiment, however one elects to measure this sentiment. Responsiveness should exist independent of the merits of the decision: people have the right to support a variety of projects, including those which public administrators might deem foolish.

Of course no system, even the most nominally democratic, allows for absolute popular mobocracy. The authors of our Constitution went to unusual lengths to make sure that when the people decided to behave foolishly they could do so only with extraordinary persistence. An appointed judiciary and a federal system were put in place to constrain democracy.

But they surely had no notion of yet another claim against the people: the need of bureaucracies for expert knowledge. The legitimacy of expert knowledge as a competing resource to popular wisdom came later, during the reform movement at the turn of the century. From Woodrow Wilson's famous essay in 1887, through the growth of scientific management, and well into the 1930s, the notion of a professional ideology was nurtured. Surely Luther Gulick and Lyndall Urwick's *Papers on the Science of Administration* (Gulick and Urwick 1937) will live in infamy. How many city managers and other students of public administration learned that POSD-CORB (Planning, Organizing, Staffing, Directing, Coordinating, Reporting, Budgeting) would solve their problems? Silly as this sort of writing sounds now, it was the foundation of the idea of "neutral competence." Experts were to be politically neutral, but technically competent. Hence, they should be shielded from the winds of public opinion. But the neutral expert never was said, even by the most rabid of the scientific managers, to be unconstrained by public choice. The belief in *unconstrained* neutral competence came later, and was more a product of the educational reform movement than of the larger municipal reform movement.

The provision of a single service affords more justification for the importance of expert knowledge to educational governance than is true in other units of local government. City managers are responsible for police and fire protection, planning, and a variety of other municipal functions. They are not expected to understand the details of each, and rely instead upon bureau chiefs. If there is any expertise commonly associated with the job of managers, it is in budgeting. As director of a multiservice government, city managers tend to be educated more broadly than superintendents, and are less likely to acquire specialized advanced degrees. Additionally, their patterns of recruitment vary more.

Schools, however, are supposed to do only one thing: educate children. Superintendents, whatever their proclivities, are expected to be able to deliver this service efficiently. The delivery of this single service is especially vulnerable to claims of expertise, since it deals with the sacred object of the child. Whereas citizens may only occasionally become excited about planning or police protection, there is so much emotion associated with the treatment of one's offspring, and consequently so much importance attached to education as the key to getting ahead, that citizens more willingly accept the legitimacy of claims for expertise in education. This is not to say, of course, that the average consumers of education are interested in the nuances of technological jargon; rather the acceptance of technology is facilitated when the object of treatment is sacred. Citizens can challenge expertise more easily when enraged about potholes than when bothered by lack of achievement. Just as the high stakes promote deference, however, they also keep the experts dangerously close to the perceived threat of lay participation. The sacred object/single service characteristics of education also increase the possibility of antiexpert backlash.

Pluralist democracy is in conflict with beliefs about administrative efficiency. As Yates (1982) argues, the institutions of pluralism involve, at a minimum, "multiple centers of power and competition" (p. 17). In city politics, whatever the private thoughts of city managers, the institutions are in place. There are mayors, city council members, relatively independent bureaucracies, and interest groups. While both managers and superintendents are children of reform movements, the very nature of a city government precludes the passion for efficiency from becoming dominant. Multiple tasks must be accomplished, and there are relatively objective ways of assessing performance. Hence, fire departments, police departments, planning departments, and the like, build their own coalitions with interest groups, city council members, and other bureaucracies. It is no coincidence that the older and more politically entrenched cities along the Eastern seaboard and in the industrial Midwest are unlikely to have a manager/council form of government. The powerful coalitions in these cities make the prospect of exercising administrative expertise untenable.

Educational governance presents a contrasting picture. There are no quasi-autonomous bureaucracies. The structure of government is hierarchical, with the superintendent responsible for delivery of a single service. While superintendents can become dependent upon their central office staffs for information, they cannot be challenged by any stable coalition of bureaucracies and interest groups.

An organization in which the primary commodity is technology should be organized hierarchically (Dahl and Lindblom 1953). If there is a technology, a "treatment," then those who receive the treatment should have minimal opportunity to assess its value. Those in possession of technology should make decisions. They should decide when, under what conditions, and with whom they will consult, if outside advice is required. They should not be responsive to nonexpert opinion. The major norms for decision making are the professional values and expertise of the administrative staff. Ideas for change, innovation, and alternative decision-making modes come through professional communication channels (Tucker and Zeigler 1980). Hence, the most frequent (and valued) communication in such organizations is internal.

When the goals of the organization are technological and the organization is hierarchical, it is reasonable to assume a degree of efficiency in the delivery of services. At the local level, police departments (although occasionally subject to demands for some lay review of policy) generally are insulated from systematic public input. Planning departments, while they hold public hearings and consult with appointed lay boards, rarely are subject to demands for responsiveness. In these organizations, especially the latter, the norm of expertise values autonomy as a positive virtue.

Planning staffs typically develop a master or comprehensive plan that seeks to anticipate needs before they are expressed. Planners, once trained primarily as engineers and landscape architects, now direct their attention to population projections, economic conditions, social patterns, life styles, cultural developments, education, transportation, and aesthetics (Dye 1969). There is a clear comparison to be drawn between planning and education. Initially, planning departments were semi-independent commissions, not subject to control by elected officials. This semi-independent status was a reflection of the aspirations of the late nineteenth- and twentieth-century reformers to remove planning from "politics." As will become apparent, much the same ideology was responsible for the governmental organization of education. However, unlike educational governance, the planning function has been institutionally reunited, slowly and irreversibly, with the political process. The trend has been to reduce the insulation of planning by making planners directly responsible to the elected mayor or council. The specific goal is to make planners less confident about technology and more sensitive about community values. While the planner's desire to take a detached and long-range view would presumably be jeopardized, a broader perspective would be achieved (Davidoff 1965). This institutional arrangement has not necessarily been successful. It is instructive to observe, however, that unlike education, the local planning function is being consciously moved into the mainstream of political life, with its attendant conflict.

The Motives of Experts

The motives of experts frequently are misunderstood and assumed to be more sinister than they actually are. Bureaucracies, staffed by experts, are said to be wresting power from legislatures in a variety of policy arenas. The explanation most frequently offered for this development is that of bureaucratic aggrandizement, or power-hungry bureaucrats. In fact, bureaucrats are not power hungry; rather they are professionally motivated to apply expert knowledge, whether or not the society wants the use of that knowledge. Bureaucrats in education and other policy arenas generally do not seek power for its own sake; they seek instead to impose on the public their professional judgments about desirable outcomes—even over the objections of lay persons who do not share their values.

The problem of expertise and political control is illustrated well by the role of public health officers and the controversy over

fluoridation of water. The job description of most public health officers (especially those serving local health authorities) requires that
they inform the public about the best available technology in the
prevention of disease. Federal grants for dissemination programs in
venereal disease, alcohol abuse, and the like, are received routinely
and are administered by such officers. Most of them believe that
fluoridation of water reduces dental problems; thus, their job requires that they distribute profluoridation material. They are genuinely puzzled when antifluoridation groups are enraged at the use of
public funds for the dissemination of such information. They must,
so they believe, resist lay efforts to constrain their behavior. The
motivation is not a lust for power, but a sincere effort to do good. In
the eyes of experts, those who resist are not in possession of adequate information. Once such information is available, they believe
that resistance will dissipate. When it does not, experts believe that
lay persons are behaving irrationally.

The distinction between "doing good" and seeking power is
essential. The temptation to accept the latter motivation is compelling, but flawed. In discussing the rise of expertise as a political resource, Gouldner regards the "new class" as "self seeking," using
its "special knowledge to advance its own interests and power, and
to control its own work situation" (Gouldner 1979, p. 82). However,
a more benign view, as, for example, advanced by Galbraith, still
allows us to view professional educational administrators (and other
public professionals) as holding the belief that they are under the
nominal control of those incompetent to judge their performances.
Autonomy, and its attendant commitment to insulation from political demands, requires that lay control be denounced as "irrational"
when such control challenges the best available technology. Again,
Gouldner argues that experts feel contempt for their lay superiors
because "they are not competent participants in the careful dis-
course concerning which technical decisions are made" (Gouldner
1979, p. 86).

The Dangers of Evangelism

Not only do schools embrace the goals of the reform movement
with more vigor than do cities, they also are more responsive to
technologies and fads, as long as they are presented as being the

product of professionally generated, technologically sophisticated processes. Today's expertise is less an expertise of scientific management than a more generalized commitment to the notion that innovations, created professionally, are preferable to responsive policies based upon the values of local consumers of education. The nexus between research and administration is closer in education than in other fields. The physical exchange of personnel between universities and school districts is not matched by any other public profession. Additionally, the federal government, through the National Institute of Education, funds a variety of projects geared toward improving education. The upshot of this nexus (universities, school districts, and the federal government) is a renewed faith by administrators in the value of applied research.

Obviously, administrators believe that schools educate their clients. More importantly, they believe that applied research can be used to solve a variety of problems in school-community relations. Scientific management lives under a variety of new names. Perhaps because of the insecurity of their professionalism, administrators are impressed by the allure of federally funded projects to assist them in problem solving. Thus, team teaching, organizational development, individualized instruction, the development of communication skills, networking, and any number of panaceas are funded and enthusiastically embraced by administrators. They want to be part of a research technology; they need the comfort of professionalism. One curious consequence of this vulnerability to fads is the existence of an extraordinarily large body of consultants.

Other governments use consultants, but generally with regard to legitimately professional problems. Consulting engineers, for example, are used by municipalities in achieving compliance with state and federal guidelines concerning water and air pollution. They rarely employ consultants in staff development, nor do they allow cadres to be created within municipal administration to evangelize about a particular innovation. Educational governance is preyed upon by consultants who specialize in rational problem solving, conflict management, or whatever the federal government is funding. It is not accidental that federal funding of proposed methods of making schools more accountable to their clientele receives less support than projects of a less politically threatening nature. States seeking to impose minimum competency tests upon the graduates of public schools have found the federal well relatively dry.

The Legacy of Reform

Technical expertise is often perceived to be in conflict with lay participation, and the resolution of this conflict has become a central concern of social scientists. For political scientists, the emergence of experts as dominant actors in the policy process is a phenomenon that presents a serious challenge to the tenets of pluralist democracy. This phenomenon causes us to continually pose the question, Who governs? For sociologists, the dilemma is one of social control. As Etzioni (1964) argues, increasing bureaucratization and professionalization make it likely that those who consume the services of schools (the public) will become even more divorced from those who provide the services (teachers and directors). For organizational analysts, conflicts surrounding participation take on an additional dimension—the tension that exists between bureaucracy and professionalism. The value of professionals in organizations is measured by their mastery of specialized knowledge. It makes sense that professionals zealously guard their claims to expertise to affirm their value to, and consequently their right to autonomy and authority in, bureaucracies. As members of the bureaucracy posture among themselves to gain liberties in their work, the public becomes an even more distant cousin to policy decisions.

The tension between experts and lay persons in the federal government accelerated as the federal government began to commit more of its resources toward domestic programs. As the administrative state emerged from the social programs of the 1960s, the difficulty of exerting congressional control became apparent. Yet rarely was the legitimacy of congressional oversight of administration challenged in its efforts to check the almost natural bureaucratic drive toward independence and autonomy. Congress not only has developed the mechanisms that it employs, but has given the president substantial statutory and procedural powers over federal administrative agencies (Dodd and Schott 1979). This is not to suggest, of course, that these mechanisms are successful; but that there is virtually no dissent from the view that they *should* be successful. As Wilensky puts it, "Although the unchecked expert represents a danger to democracy and efficiency, the danger can be constrained by the training of executives, the use of adversary safeguards and similar administrative devices and the force of an enlightened public opinion" (Wilensky 1967, p. 116).

None of the tensions between experts and representatives is unique. All governments in complex societies are vulnerable to bureaucratic dominance. The intransigent bureaucracy, among other distractions, drove Mr. Nixon to despair. Subsequently, his Republican successor promised to reduce the size and impact of federal bureaucracy, and to return a variety of government functions to states and municipalities (where, unbeknownst to him, they would become the creatures of equally odious bureaucracies). Reagan's antibureaucratic bent struck a responsive chord: nobody likes faceless bureaucrats.

Local politics differ from national politics, however, because they are reformed, especially in medium-sized and smaller areas. The reform movement nicked the state government a bit with its various referenda schemes, but it was in local politics that the reformers had their greatest success. The infamous urban machines were corrupt, as the reformers alleged. They were not efficient, if the word is understood to mean providing the best service for the least money. But, as most students of the period have concluded, the urban machines performed an essential function. In integrating the millions of immigrants into political life, they rewarded votes with jobs. Their currency was patronage. To reformers, giving a teacher a job because he or she had paid off a ward boss was so horrible a crime as to require a massive reorganization. The idea was to let professional rather than political criteria determine the course of local government. The goal was efficiency, a word that became the gospel of the reformers. Efficiency requires expertise. Experts require autonomy. Hence, the reform movement required the appointment of technically competent experts who, in turn, would assure their elected employers that services were being delivered efficiently.

Both educational and municipal structures of governance have been shaped by the forces of local governmental reform in the early part of this century, and school and municipal decision makers today have many issues, problems, and constraints in common. Just as the council-manager form of government often is identified as one of the goals of municipal reform, so was the modern school superintendency a product of educational reform (Banfield and Wilson 1966; Boynton 1976; Dye 1973). Municipal and school district reforms were guided by the same tripartite ideology:

1. A belief in the "public interest," which should prevail over competing, partial interests. This belief was reflected in slogans such as "There is no Republican or Democrat way to pave a street." In the educational field the slogan was "There is no Republican or Democrat way to school a child."

2. Since reasonable men can agree on the public interest, government is really an administrative and technical problem, rather than a political one. Politics is the art of decision making most appropriate when there is disagreement concerning goals. Since municipal and educational governance issues are amenable to consensual decision making by "reasonable" people, both politics and "unreasonable" people should be barred from the decision-making process.

3. The best qualified people should decide on policy and then leave the administration of programs to professional experts. Institutional arrangements should guarantee both the selection of those best qualified for positions of lay leadership and the provision of a corps of professional experts to shoulder the burden of administration.

This common ideology gave rise to common institutional arrangements in school districts and council-manager municipal governments. Six key structural changes were sought and largely achieved:

1. Bypassing party machinery in nominations and elections. Nonpartisan selection of legislators, recall of legislators, and direct citizen participation through referenda and other plebiscites were the prime structural changes.

2. Reduction of elective offices to simplify the voter's task (the "short ballot") and to focus responsibility on a small number of top elected officials.

3. Replacement of ward-based elections with at-large elections to insure that elected officials would consider the welfare of the entire governmental unit and not merely their own neighborhoods or "wards."

4. Longer, overlapping terms for legislators to ensure continuing availability of expertise and proper socialization of newcomers.

5. Separation of local politics by holding elections at times when there are no federal or state elections.

6. Replacement of patronage appointment and promotion of employees by a merit system of civil service.

Of course, not all school districts or council-manager municipal governments have all of these institutional structures. However, the structures characterize the overwhelming majority of local school districts (Zeigler and Jennings 1974; Tucker and Zeigler 1978). Moreover, these institutional structures are strongly associated with the council-manager form of municipal government—more so than with any other form of municipal government.

A brief review of data on school district and council-manager institutions will serve to document how similar are these two forms of local government. As Table 1.1 indicates, the council-manager form of local government has grown over the past 30 years to become the most common form of government in cities of 5,000 or more in population. Table 1.1 also indicates that the council-manager form has been growing at the expense of both the mayor-council and commission forms, and that the council-manager and mayor-council forms account for 93 percent of city governments.

The reform goal of nonpartisan selection of lay legislators has been achieved in both school districts and council-manager municipalities. Approximately 25 percent of all school districts select board members by partisan election (Zeigler and Jennings 1974). As Table 1.2 indicates, council-manager cities have the lowest rate of partisan elections. Less than 13 percent of council-manager municipalities allow partisan electoral competition.

Ward-based election of legislative officials has been curtailed in both school districts and municipal governments. About 73 percent of school districts have pure, at-large elections (Zeigler and Jennings 1974). Of the 49 largest cities surveyed by the National School Boards Association, 82 percent of school districts that elect

Table 1.1   Form of City Government in Cities of 5,000 or More (in percentages)

	Mayor-Council	Council-Manager	Com-mission	Town Meeting	Representa-tive Town Meeting	Sample Size
1951	55.0	26.1	15.3	2.5	1.1	2,525
1953	52.7	28.9	14.7	2.6	1.1	2,527
1957	49.4	34.6	12.5	2.3	1.2	2,559
1959	48.3	36.3	12.1	2.0	1.2	2,562
1963	52.3	38.6	8.1	0.4	0.6	3,044
1967	48.6	41.2	6.1	2.9	1.2	3,113
1971	44.0	47.3	5.9	1.8	1.1	1,875
1974	46.0	47.1	3.0	*	*	6,254
1978	44.0	46.0	3.0	*	*	8,192

*Breakdown not available.

Source: The Municipal Year Book, 1952, 1954, 1958, 1960, 1964, 1968, 1972, 1976, 1978. (Washington, D.C.: International City Management Association).

**Table 1.2   Cities with Partisan Affiliation on General
Election Ballots (in percentages)**

	All	Mayor-Council	Council-Manager	Com-mission	Town Meeting	Representa-tive Town Meeting
1951	40.6	54.7	15.4	33.3	48.9	20.8
1953	39.8	54.6	15.6	34.3	52.0	25.0
1957	39.0	56.0	15.0	37.0	49.0	20.0
1959	39.0	56.0	16.0	39.0	55.0	23.0
1963	36.0	51.0	16.0	37.0	46.0	24.0
1967	35.1	50.8	17.7	30.5	43.5	39.3
1974	24.5	35.8	12.8	17.4	41.2	24.3

Source: The Municipal Year Book, 1952, 1954, 1958, 1960, 1964, 1968, 1976.
(Washington, D.C.: International City Management Association).

board members do so on an at-large basis (National School Boards Association 1975). Over the last quarter century, three-fourths of council-manager municipalities have consistently elected city council members on an at-large basis.

Despite a common origin, when educational and municipal administrators are confronted with the task of managing conflict, they respond differently because of their personal and professional resources and administrative positions. The disparity suggests the logic and utility of comparative research for understanding the conflict management behavior of local administrators.

Some research has treated the role of conflict management behavior for city managers in municipal governance (Eyestone 1971; Loveridge 1971; Stillman 1974). But conflict as an area of inquiry is still novel to educational research. Salisbury (1980), in his recent study of citizen participation in education, notes his surprise at the recurrence of conflict throughout the course of his interviews. Salisbury's conclusions are highly revealing:

> School activists dislike conflict. They are uneasy about political parties because, in part at least, partisan involvement implies directly competitive struggle. They are uneasy about changes within their communities or in their school program, in part it seems, because change presents the possibility of disagreement. They are, with some exceptions, uneasy in the presence of heterogeneity, of race or class, because this too means potential conflict over what values ought to prevail. . . . Our data are

not remotely sufficient to explore thoroughly this issue, but the matter of American attitudes toward political and social conflict is thoroughly deserving of a prominent place in the research agenda (Salisbury 1980, pp. 198–99).

Comparative analysis would have eased Salisbury's concern; we give conflict "a prominent place in the research agenda."

This concern with constraining experts is not widely shared by professional educators. Rather, their interest is in the assurance that professionals are unconstrained. Indeed, the ideology of educational administration, as it emerged from the reform movement at the turn of the century, was one that emphasized "expertise, professionalization, non-political control, and efficiency" (Wirt and Kirst 1972). In their view, the best guarantee of a well-functioning school system is in the free exercise of judgment by highly trained experts. Havinghurst, asserting that the role of experts in large city school administrations was dominant only until 1970, argues that the goal of quality education for all can be achieved only by a "strong school administration, with power over a wide population area . . . with a strong planning function, and with a bureaucracy" (Havinghurst 1977, p. 105).

Other arenas of policy have a cadre of experts. Indeed, the rapid rate at which the United States is changing, out of necessity, from a political/economic system concerned with the distribution of abundant resources to one virtually obsessed with the conservation of scarce resources makes expertise a highly valued commodity. However, education seems to be a public enterprise that places an unusual amount of value upon deference to experts, whether or not such experts can legitimately claim to live up to their titles.

In spite of the intervention of federal and state authorities in local governance, the local administrative structure, symbolized by the superintendent, remains the most visible and influential unit in educational governance. In most districts, school boards are part-time amateur bodies easily persuaded that superintendents are better equipped than they to make policy. The superintendent is the single most visible representative of the school system. The average citizen more readily can name his or her superintendent of schools than his or her congressional representative, to say nothing of elected school board members. The average superintendent earns more than the average city manager, for example, and presides over a larger bureaucracy. In spite of the fact that schools are responsible for the delivery of a single service—education—their ratio of auxillary personnel to service delivery personnel exceeds that of any other unit of local government. For this and other reasons, schools are the largest single consumer of local tax dollars. Hence, the popular identification of schools with superintendents is understandable.

Why A Comparison?

There are those who assert that we will find few differences between school superintendents and city managers. Stillman (1974), for example, has claimed that "public school superintendents have a great deal in common with city managers. Both are administrators of important community enterprises; both are at the beck and call of local boards, both face similar problems of general public apathy and wrath over local issues (frequently at budget time), and both enjoy comparable remunerations for their services." Cognizant of such commonalities, the International City Managers Association and the American Association of School Administrators in 1963 and 1964 held a series of joint conferences to explore similarities between the two professions, options for training, and problems of administration.

These similarities aside, we expect that there are significant differences between the two groups in conflict management behavior. Although few studies of comparative conflict management within the same general geographical unit exist, we can explicate what differences we expect to exist. Comparative analysis should be undertaken when the units to be studied have an appropriate mix of similarities and differences—comparisons of totally disparate cultures (Iceland and New Caledonia) or quite similar cultures (Alabama and Georgia) should be avoided.

The point is well illustrated by the varieties of settings in which conflicts can occur. There are conflicts in families, organizations, social movements, and nation-states. Although these settings for conflict differ substantially, there are still opportunities to generalize. Formal organizations and nations are the two entities that yield the most efforts at comparative analysis. A state has a legitimate monopoly over coercion while an organization does not. On the other hand, formal organizations usually have clearly defined goals whereas nations rarely do. Conflict in formal organization can be ephemeral or stable, while conflict in nations tends to endure for generations, transmitted through class systems and families. Nevertheless, nations and organizations are two settings from which our understanding of conflict is enhanced by comparison.

The differences between city managers and superintendents, perhaps less extreme, nevertheless offer an ideal opportunity for a comparative study of conflict management. These differences are described below.

Professionalism. A key ingredient of professionalism is autonomy, the freedom to make decisions about one's work. The stronger the sense of professionalism, the greater the need for autonomy. In addition to our own work, Schumpeter (1942) was among the first to understand the impact of education upon the need for professional autonomy. Most city managers are administrative generalists, most superintendents are selected from within educational ranks. The educational backgrounds of city managers are diverse; the education of superintendents, more narrow and specialized. Superintendents normally possess more formal educational credentials than city managers; most have advanced degrees. Studies of graduate curricula in educational administration further indicate that course work is highly specialized.

Thus, we believe there is a higher sense of *professional identification* among superintendents than among managers, and that this identification, although it may enhance intraorganizational authority, is dysfunctional in the resolution of community conflicts that expand to the point where expertise is no longer a valued resource. As Mosher has pointed out, "It is doubtful that there is any element . . . more significant for the nature of its public service than the educational system, both formal and informal, by which are transmitted its other frame of reference, and knowledge, and partly through which these are changed and knowledge enlarged" (1982, p. 25).

One city manager, reflecting upon his training and his job experiences, lamented, "the would-be manager is trained as a managerial generalist, uncontaminated by any taint of political craft. . . ." He went on to argue that "profession" does not describe the manager's job, *"and it would be a disaster if it did."* On the other hand, "making the manager a better politician is advocated, even to the extent of engaging personally in the electoral process" (Donaldson 1973, pp. 505–6). Such opinions are not part of the ideology of superintendents, although results discussed in the next chapter suggest a gap between espoused ideology and present day attitudes of superintendents when queried individually.

Scope of Public Goods. Just as the educational background of superintendents is more concentrated than that of managers, so the public good they distribute is more limited. Managers are responsible for the administration of a broad range of services; superintendents, a single service. Further, the service provided by superintendents involves a "sacred object," the child. Most of the services directed by city managers do not involve objects of such emotional attachment. Planning and budgeting for municipal services seem to involve more pragmatic than ideological bargaining. This is not to say, of course, that ideological conflict is absent. The literature on fluoridation and the widespread attention given to the treatment of homosexuals demonstrate that, indeed, it is very present. Further, even a cursory examination of urban life suggests that central city problems are becoming *less* technical. In this sense, the problems of city manager and superintendent are similar: the problems are becoming less amenable to technical solutions, yet the recruitment of managers and superintendents still favors the technical problem solvers (Stillman 1974, p. 107). Banfield and Wilson contend that ". . . managers as a class are better at assembling and interpreting technical data, analyzing the logic of a problem, and applying rules to particular cases than they are at sensing the complications of a human situation" (1963, p. 174).

Role as Policy Initiator. City managers, like superintendents, now are expected to initiate policy. Both were initially regarded as neutral experts, a clearly untenable role. Both now are viewed as having broader responsibilities. Past research leaves no doubt about the role of the superintendent (Zeigler and Jennings 1974; Tucker and Zeigler 1980). Research on city managers (Loveridge 1971; Eyestone 1971) reaches similar conclusions for managers. Indeed, Kammerer's analysis of publications of the International City Manager's Association from 1952–62 reveals more references to the role of policy leader or innovator than to any other role (1964, p. 428).

However, important differences are present. City councils represent a more diverse range of religious, educational, and financial backgrounds than do school boards (Eulau and Prewitt 1973; Torgovnik 1969, p. 35). Deference to expertise is more characteristic of middle- to upper-class professionals than of less affluent social classes. Thus, the city manager's role in policy formation is more likely to be challenged by the city council than is the superintendent's by the board, especially when the council is led by an active, popularly elected mayor. Kammerer observed that city managers had less range of discretion under these circumstances (1964, p. 439). A direct comparison can be made with one of the cities in an earlier study (Tucker and Zeigler 1980) in which the mayor became, by reason of his office, chairman of the school board. In this case, superintendent discretion was limited.

Alliances and Interest Groups. Partially because of their more general and substantive managerial responsibilities, city managers face the problem of alliances between department leaders and organized interest groups. The executive bureau-interest group relationship so well documented in the interest group literature on national politics (Truman 1951; Zeigler and Peak 1972) is becoming characteristic of large urban political systems. Thus, managers might find themselves in conflict with heads of administrative agencies in alliance with their clientele groups. This phenomenon is less often found in school governance although superintendents must, of necessity, rely on staff for information. The governance structure does not encourage administrative-interest group alliances independent of the superintendent.

However, superintendent relations with school principals creates problems not felt by city managers. Whereas municipal departments develop strong relations with functional interest groups, principals may develop independent influence based upon geographical identification.

Principals and teachers are in positions to contain or exacerbate conflict by implementation. As Majone and Wildavsky (1973) argue, it is clear that implementation shapes policy. That is, the impact of a policy upon the intended public will be subject to manipulation by the line officials. The extent to which principals correctly interpret the values of their constituents and make incremental adjustments in policy will be an important variable in conflict resolution.* Securing the loyalty of principals—and allowing them the latitude to modify policy—can be a valuable strategy for superintendents.

The fact that such buffer opportunities are not as available for city managers may create more direct group interaction and conflict with politically influential elites.

---

*We are grateful to Harry Wolcott, Richard Carlson, and W. W. Charters, Jr. for assisting us on this point.

Thus, the opportunities for comparison are ideal: Martin notes, "Observers of the municipal and school scene have commented on the similarity of roles of city managers and school superintendents and have suggested that specimens of each be dissected and compared. School administrators and city managers themselves have commented on these similarities and have even compared salaries as a guide to standards of compensation." He also states, " . . . all school districts and a large and growing number of cities operate under systems which are comparable in many important respects . . . that the students of public education and city government might learn much from cross analysis would seem so obvious as to require no documentation" (1967, p. 41).

To summarize then, the bases for expected differences in the way city managers and superintendents deal with conflict include the following:

1. Superintendents' stronger sense of professional identification is a disadvantage in handling expanded conflicts, where expertise is not as relevant a resource as in intraorganizational disputes.
2. The difference in the scope and nature of the "public goods" superintendents and city managers administer implies that the two groups will need different skills to deal with conflict. The mix of technical and ideological conflict is characteristically different for each group, and so the most effective mix of skills also will vary.
3. Managers and superintendents have different roles as policy initiators, and have different relationships with their elected councils/boards. Conflict management styles will vary according to the parties to the conflict.
4. Municipal government is functionally decentralized, and the school system is geographically decentralized. Consequently, managers and superintendents confront different kinds of alliances between subordinates and clientele groups. Heads of municipal departments develop strong relations with functional interest groups, and principals develop geographic bases of influence.

The addiction of administrators to technical knowledge is well grounded in the curriculum of schools of education. Although superintendents are told that they are politicians, the emphasis in educational administration is upon the tradition of rational management. Nowhere is the distinction between rational management and political decision making clearer than in the approach to conflict. A political view of conflict emphasizes that conflict is healthy; a management point of view is based upon the assumption that conflict is symptomatic of a "breakdown in the standard mechanism of decision-making and 'a threat' to cooperation" (March and Simon 1964). A political approach to conflict has a much more benign view: "Political conflict is not an unfortunate and temporary aberration from the norm of perfect harmony and cooperation. It stems from the very character of human life itself" (Ranney 1966).

Not only is conflict normal, it is, according to the political view, healthy rather than pathological: "The dynamo of political action, meaningful conflict, produces engaged leaders, who in turn generate more conflict among the people. Conflict relevant to popular aspirations is also the key democratizer of leadership" (Burns 1978). The key distinction, of course, is between normal politics and the administrative rationality based upon the traditional assumption that education and politics do not mix. Keeping education out of politics means eliminating conflict. The typical administrator, then, will regard conflict as destructive noise in the system. It must be managed; it must be anticipated, contained, individualized, controlled, and, if possible, avoided.

Superintendents attend workshops at which strategies for rational conflict management are displayed in much the same fashion that physicians attend seminars on the early detection of life-threatening diseases. Superintendents learn from consultants that, for example, traditional political assumptions are dangerous. Conflict assumes that somebody wins and somebody loses. Politicians try to minimize the effects of losing, but all decisions, no matter how carefully the compromise is drawn, necessarily involve winners and losers. Such is the nature of politics. Superintendents, however, are encouraged to believe that conflict can be eliminated by "win-win" decisions. That is, they believe that it is possible to make decisions in which everybody wins, thus eliminating conflict. Such solutions are to be accomplished by the appropriate training of potential participants.

In the next chapter we examine traditional perceptions of conflict and how it should be managed. The analysis of similarities and differences in the way superintendents and city managers approach conflict management yields implications for effective behavior in both settings. Beyond conflict management behavior, the comparison illuminates the degree to which these two groups of professionals are responsive to their publics and where the locus of decision making resides.

—2—

Conflict

Traditional Views of Conflict

While managers in municipal governance have always operated in a traditional political context, such conditions have been considered to be the exception for school managers. However, the turbulence of the 1960s certainly seemed to have affected the conditions of education and contributed to its politicization. Popular accounts of highly publicized conflicts portrayed professionals as struggling vainly against a variety of powerful interest groups. Professionals themselves were active in promulgating the view of the "beleaguered superintendent" (Boyd 1975, p. 7). One observer from the ranks of the beleaguered quoted the following to support his contention that the world of the superintendent, as seen from the inside, is far more conflictual than the world as described by students of educational policy making:

> The American school superintendent, long the benevolent ruler whose word was law, has become a harried, embattled figure of waning authority. . . browbeaten by once subservient boards of education, teachers' associations, and parents, the superintendent can hardly be blamed if he feels he has lost control of his destiny. . . . Administrative powerlessness is becoming one of the most pervasive realities of organizational life (Maeroff 1975, p. 1; Erickson 1972, pp. 3–4).

While some might be inclined to dismiss such testimony as self-serving, the view has been to some extent echoed by scholars who argue that the model of professional dominance is no longer operative. Representative of this argument is McCarty and Ramsey's *The School Managers* (1971). This study of 51 school districts in the Northeast and Midwest led them to conclude:

> One can hardly avoid the view that today's educational administrator is engulfed in a pressure packed set of constraints . . . individuals previously without power are rapidly becoming aware of the strength that can be marshalled if they work together . . . the tensions so apparent throughout American society have galvanized [school] boards into the political arena with a vengeance (McCarty and Ramsey 1971, pp. 153, 211, and 213).

The upshot of this controversy has been a renewed interest in the question: Are schools really that conflictual? This new interest is shared by practitioners and scholars in educational administration, political science, sociology, and other social sciences. Social scientists who see a technological revolution as changing the basis of governmental decision making are interested in exploring the technological decision-making model so well established in the educational policy literature. Simultaneously, students and practitioners of educational administration who see increasing politicization of educational governance are interested in exploring topics such as popular participation and conflict resolution under the democratic decision-making model (Boyd 1976b, pp. 539–77). All of these perspectives need to be explored to resolve the apparent contradiction between research findings that show professional administrators dominating the processes of educational policy making with the assertion of "schoolmen themselves or observers sympathetic to them that they have lost control of the governing of schools" (Boyd 1975; Wirt and Christovich 1982).

We suggest that the resolution to the problem lies in greater understanding of educational policy making under conditions of conflict in which the technological model of decision making most often is challenged as inappropriate, in which the democratic model has a chance to operate, and which seems to be particularly trying for school administrators. The major purpose of this writing is to further understandings of conflict management in educational governance.

Contrary to the professional maxim that superintendents should not engage in politics, superintendents are political actors with political powers. As in other units of government, school district governance involves conflict. For many superintendents, political conflict presents a crucial paradox: when conflict occurs, the technical skills so diligently developed not only are of no value, they are a liability. Trained in the tenets of an ideology that defines conflict as pathological and consensus as the most legitimate basis of a decision, superintendents may find conflict more painful than do other executive officers. A defensive, hostile response to criticism then may generate more intense conflict. Thus, superintendents with doctoral degrees (the most ideologically committed) and little on-the-job experience (which mediates the negative influence of education) may be less skillful in managing conflict (Crain 1968, pp. 115–24; Boss, Zeigler, Tucker, and Wilson 1976). Boss, Zeigler, Tucker, and Wilson (1976) showed that those with doctorates were less successful in managing conflict than those without this advanced degree.

Problems concerning conflict resolution are especially acute under conditions of episodic, nonroutinized conflict. Episodic conflict reduces the effectiveness of the basic resources of the manager. The basic resource of superintendents, expertise, is not accepted as negotiable. Because superintendents rely on expertise rather than more traditional political skills, the power base of the superintendent is destroyed when this resource is declared inapplicable. It is no surprise that issues of episodic conflict unresolvable by technical skills (such as busing and school closures made necessary by declining enrollments) are troublesome to superintendents. As U.S. schools move from an era of expanding resources to one of scarce resources, the essentially political issue of resource distribution will become dominant. School boards will continue to turn to superintendents for recommendations. Superintendents must use both their political and technical resources as the task of conflict management becomes more prominent in school district governance.

Systematic research should not focus exclusively on those instances in which the technological mode of decision making is inappropriate (i.e., examples of nonroutine, or episodic, conflict). However, such instances are important beyond their numbers; they provide opportunities for implementing the democratic mode of decision making. Peterson, Boyd, Zald, and others have suggested this possibility. As Zald explains: "It is at such times, too, that basic conflicts and diversions both with the board and between the managers and the board are likely to be pronounced" (Boyd 1975, p. 107). Boyd argues that such occasions concern, for example, finance and

expansion, school consolidation, and the selection of new superintendents (1975, p. 121). However, the evidence is far from clear.
Our own research indicates that there is more involved than the substance of the issue, a point that we will develop in a later section of
this text.

A Definition of Conflict

Conflict has been the source of conceptual confusion for decades (Fink 1968). We have sifted through definitions ranging from
the most basic to the most complex. Introductory texts in political
science simply define conflict as "situations in which one individual
wishes to follow a line of action that would make it difficult or impossible for someone else to pursue his own desires" (Dahl 1981). Such
texts also assume the necessity, indeed the desirability, of conflict.
More sophisticated conceptual schemes, such as proposed by
Schmidt and Kochan (1972), include not only goal incompatibility
but also a variety of other preconditions. That is, they agree that
incompatibility of goals is a necessary, but not a sufficient, definition
of conflict.

We start with a generally accepted definition: conflict is a situation in which two or more parties perceive that their goals are incompatible. Obviously, conflict is common in schools or in any organization (Nebgen 1978). However, perceived incompatibility of
goals may not lead to behavior normally regarded as conflictual.
One school of thought—derived initially from the early work of Ross
(1930) and Simmel (1955)—argues that incompatible goals may lead
either to conflict or competition. The difference between these is
analogous to the difference between a race and a fight. In a race,
nothing is done normally to obstruct one's opponents' efforts,
whereas, in a fight, obstruction is the goal. The fight is a social phenomenon and includes an element of interaction. Lewis Coser's definition of social conflict is applicable; he describes it as "A struggle
over values and claims to scarce status, power and resources in
which the aims of the opponents are to neutralize, injure or eliminate their rivals (1956, p. 8).

Thus, our definition expands to include: mutually perceived
and incompatible goals, and perceived opportunity for interference.
Stated in terms of traditional social science, conflict consists of situ-

ations in which persons with perceived mutually incompatible goals simultaneously perceive an *opportunity* to achieve these goals (at least partially) by *blocking* those of their adversaries. This additional active component, the blocking behavior of opponents, constitutes a refinement of our earlier distinctions between active and passive conflict and is helpful in sharpening our understanding of management behavior.

Having provided a definition capable of being operationalized, our next task is to specify the *dimensions* of conflict. Following Sorokin (1927), the literature traditionally approaches this task by identifying the nature of the antagonistic unity. Our review of the literature reveals dozens of schemes, each with a domain of social science attached to it. At the extreme, some works, like those of Boulding (1962), classify parties of conflicts from personal to international. While such efforts admittedly are tedious, they should not be overlooked as each has attracted the attention of various teams of social scientists. Thus, personal quarrels attract the attention of small-group psychologists while conflicts between nation-states interest students of international relations.

Clearly we can eliminate many types of conflict that administrators may encounter. Any private conflicts, for example, are not of concern to us. (Of course, one can always argue that a manager's private conflicts affect his/her public behavior, but we suspect that the theory here is too murky; see Rogow and Lasswell 1963.) Our analysis of the literature, including the work of Dahrendorf (1959), Boulding (1962), and McNeil (1965) leads to the conclusion that our purposes are best served by reduction and simplification.

Stephen K. Bailey's (1971) typology of conflict provides a beginning. He identified three types of conflict situations: subordinate conflict (between an administrator and subordinates); superordinate conflict (between an administrator and superiors); and lateral conflict (between an administrator and equals).

The advantages of Bailey's typology of conflict situations are manifest in the ambiguities it suggests as well as in its simplicity. Conflict may develop because neither party agrees to the definitions of the authority relationship. Loveridge (1971), for example, finds fundamental conflict between council members and managers in their perceptions of the manager's role in policy making. Our research on boards and superintendents similarly suggests that, in some situations, the conflict involves less the substance of a dispute than an appropriate definition of the role of each actor vis-à-vis the other.

Gross, Mason, and McEachern's study (1958) of school boards in Massachusetts provided some of the theories leading to our *Governing American Schools* (1974). Gross et al. worked directly on the notion of board-superintendent conflict by using an item to measure degree of "professionalism." Their item was phrased (response terms of agreeing or disagreeing): "In deciding issues the board members vote as representatives of important blocs or segments." The model superintendent response was "Absolutely must not." Our question, based both upon Gross et al. and upon theories of representation, was: "Do you ever feel any conflict between your responsibility to the public and to the school administration?" The majority of board members did not, but in cases of conflict our analysis revealed that the dispute was, indeed, as much over appropriate roles as over substantive issues. In Bailey's terms, the disputes involved conflict over whether board-superintendent relations were subordinate, superordinate, or lateral. Bailey's typology, in addition to offering the idea that conflicts may concern the disputants' appropriate roles, offers the additional advantage of clarification of research domains.

Subordinate conflict is germane to the fields of administration, industrial relations, and related disciplines. Most literature on management (whether public or private) is concerned with managing disturbances *within* the organization, where a hierarchy of authority normally is established. Clearly, management is concerned about subordinate conflicts because the collective goals of the organization are disrupted if subordinate conflict is poorly treated. Hence, the literature quite naturally treats conflict as a destructive force. Such terms as "a breakdown in standard mechanism of decision-making" (March and Simon 1964) and "a threat to cooperation" (Marek 1966) are illustrative of this understandable assumption.

Our concern is not, of course, with subordinate disputes as such. However, our interest in them is substantive for a number of reasons: one being that unresolved subordinate disputes may result in a broadening of conflict to either the superordinate or lateral levels. Mintzberg's (1973) description of the "disturbance handler" role is representative of the management literature not only in its dysfunctional characterization ("disturbance occurs, a correction is necessary"), but also in that it does not address the possibility that

the disturbance may expand. For example, principals who feel they
have been improperly managed may seek legal redress through a
superordinate source (courts); teachers who cannot resolve a dispute may withhold their services and garner the support or opposition of community organizations, which have lateral authority relations with school managers.

An additional reason for our concern with subordinate conflicts
is the assumption, again from Mintzberg, that managers spend a
good portion of their time reacting to disturbance situations. If so,
then several research opportunities exist. At the simple descriptive
level, What kinds of conflict are most prevalent and most costly?

On the one hand, management texts (and management research, generally) are devoted to the handling of intraorganizational
disturbances. On the other hand, school managers, as we have reported elsewhere, argue that they are "administratively powerless"
because boards of education, teachers' organizations, parents, and
other community groups are becoming more active. As we have
noted, along with Boyd and with Zald, such events (if the challenge
to authority is by a lateral group) may occur only infrequently but
with major impact. Intraorganizational disputes may occur frequently but with minor impact if they are contained. Again, we note,
with modest linguistic change, another distinction between episodic
and routine conflict—intraorganizational disputes are more easily
routinized.

Since so much of the literature is concerned with the management of intraorganizational conflict, we raise here the possibility
that managers adept at handling intraorganizational disturbances
may be inept at resolving lateral conflicts. Management techniques
may vary with the type of conflict (Nebgen 1978). A reasonable hypothesis (to be developed below) is that training managers in subordinate conflicts may inhibit their ability to handle lateral conflicts.
Such an idea was suggested by Crain (1968) in discussing the response of superintendents to demands for school desegregation:
"Interaction between civil rights leaders and school superintendents has the preconditions for conflict."

The literature of political science is substantially more directed
toward lateral and superordinate conflict. Easton, whose early work
has directly or indirectly influenced most empirical and theoretical
work, clearly distinguishes between studies of organizations and
studies of "the authoritative allocations of values." His argument is

that political scientists should study policies that, broadly speaking, involve the "whole society." Hence, "political science is not interested in the power relations of a gang or a family or a church group simply because in them one man or group contests the actions of another" (Easton 1953, p. 123). Easton's argument is not, of course, that one should exclude nonpublic activity; rather he is suggesting that the purpose of inquiry is to address public policy-making behavior.

It is normal, therefore, for political scientists to be more concerned with conflict that engages the attention of broader publics than about intraorganizational disputes (keeping in mind the caveat that the lines are frequently blurred). As Dye and Hawkins explain, "Metropolitan government is too often treated as a problem in administration rather than a problem in the resolution of conflict" (1967, p. 1). Yet, according to these authors, and to others such as Banfield and Wilson (1963), "the management of conflict *in society* is one of the basic purposes of government."

The degree to which political scientists focus on societal or community conflict goes beyond Easton. Indeed, the founding fathers, especially Madison, believed that regulating conflict among people with diverse interests was the principal task of government. Madison, of course, was borrowing directly from Hobbes, who argued that totally unregulated conflict was incompatible with community life. Hobbes, Madison, and Easton all argue in diverse ways that the principal business of government is the management of societal conflicts.

However, the scope of conflict did not become focused upon the community (that is, the local community, as distinguished from larger units) until James Coleman's seminal *Community Conflict* (1957). Using fluoridation disputes as examples of conflict-laden public policies, Coleman developed an overarching theory of the conditions for community conflict: (1) the event must touch upon an important aspect of the community members' lives (here he specifically mentions education and taxes, providing support for our comparative focus); (2) the event must affect the lives of different community members differently; and (3) the event must be one about which community members feel that action can be taken.

Coleman's conditions for conflict fit nicely with our definition, as he explicitly includes the active component. One example of the condition for conflict cited by Coleman was a conflict over school taxes. Coleman argues, however, that the "real beginnings" of this conflict (which resulted in the ouster of the superintendent) could be found in the *decision-making style* of the superintendent (especially his insulation from politically active persons and groups). We share Coleman's belief in the utility of using management style as a predictor variable.

The significance of Coleman's conclusion is that he tacitly acknowledges a distinction that we have been most anxious to preserve—the distinction between unavoidable conflicts generated by the structure of the community and those triggered by an event or issue (in the case cited, the superintendent's behavior). The latter conflicts are, we believe, more amenable to manipulation as their origins may stem partially from behaviors acquired as a result of training received in courses in the field of education.

Coleman also makes note of conflicts that began because of the necessity of implementing decisions reached at another, extra-local unit of government. He argued in 1957 that community conflicts would erupt more in response to state or national decisions, that is, to the sources outside the community, as the jurisdictional shrinkage of local communities became apparent. As noted, response to external mandates often results in conflict (1957, p. 80).

Coleman's work, while theoretically elegant, was empirically sparse. However, other studies of community conflict, normally using fluoridation as an example, developed Coleman's notions more completely. Of particular relevance is the parallel between conflict over fluoridation and the various conflicts surrounding schools, since both pit experts against lay persons. The clearest exposition of this point is in Crain (1968). They emphasize that *management style* (defined as insulation from or engagement with community conflict) is an important and malleable variable.

Like many educational decisions, the fluoridation issue appears to have been *initiated* by professionals. In our terminology, initiation is equivalent to *proposal development*. Expert participation in proposal development is a major point in *The Quest for Responsive Government* (Tucker and Zeigler 1978). The authors note that, because proposal development requires the specification of a need for policy and the presentation of alternatives, "most important measures are . . . suggested by . . . administrative departments that have studied the subjects involved and are prepared to present to the legislature the information on which it may base its action. By the time the legislature, council, or school board comes into play, the issue and policy options are well defined'' (p. 137).

In the evolution of a policy, professional (as opposed to lay) participation tends to occur early. Those who specialize in the agenda-setting aspects of political participation stress the importance of early professional participation, because experts hope to avoid a conflict of expanded scope and high visibility (Cobb and Elder 1972, p. 51). Cobb and Elder, Coleman (1957), and Gamson (1966, 1968) all argue that expanded lay participation enhances the probability of conflict and that each expansion is more easily contained early in the policy process, that is, at the level of proposal development. Even when the conflict is expanded, as for example by legal requirements for a referendum, early professional activity seems a crucial ingredient in predicting the nature of resolution. Thus, there is a high correlation between a city manager's policy position and the outcome of fluoridation referenda (Crain 1968, p. 125). Even so, argues Crain, city managers prefer to define issues as administrative or noncontroversial, because their consensual style is strained by conflict (p. 205).

It can be seen from this discussion that students of community conflict rarely discuss intraorganizational conflict. Cobb and Elder are quite explicit about this, limiting their discussion for the most part to "external" conflict—that conflict characterized by efforts of contending parties to control the allocations of socially valued goods (1972, p. 39). Hence, as we did in our earlier thinking, they address themselves to the scope, intensity, and visibility of conflict. For them, the study of conflict is largely a study of the expansion of scope, the development of controversy, and the extent to which the interaction of these two variables (scope and intensity) impact upon visibility.

Our perspective is in this tradition. Social science literature presents us with a variety of phenomena under the rubric of conflict. We are most concerned with conflicts that have expanded into the arena of public policy, engaging the attention of publics outside the organization. This does not, however, preclude awareness of the consequences of intraorganizational conflict on the process of conflict expansion.

To summarize, our thinking about the kinds of conflict we wish to study encompasses these items:

1. Conflict is a situation in which two or more parties perceive that their goals are incompatible.
2. The parties to conflict also perceive opportunity to achieve their own goals (at least in part) by blocking the goals of others. That is, we are concerned with situations in which incompatible goals are actively pursued.
3. Bailey's typology of conflict situations, based on the symmetry of authority relationships, identifies subordinate, superordinate, and lateral conflicts. Organization theory focuses on subordinate (intraorganizational) conflicts. From our perspective such conflicts are ancillary to our interest in lateral and superordinate conflicts, typically the concern of political science.
4. Studies of community and organizational conflict are our main theoretical and empirical referents. The dominant theme of this literature is that the study of conflict is largely the study of the expansion of scope. An essential component of the conflicts we are interested in is the involvement of the public in the conflict situation—in some degree, to some extent, in some manner. In this view, conflict management would not be solely a matter of maintaining the structure of authority relationships within an organization, but of participation in the development of conflict in the public arena.

We believe, additionally, that organizational theory has been too simplistic in its assumptions about conflict termination. Our pretest persuades us of the merits of a less mechanistic view. Such a view is supported by the work of Lewis Coser. Coser (1961) argues that in social conflict, provisions for termination must be made by the contenders and that termination must occur in their eyes. He asserts that conflict is not terminated unless all parties recognize that the conflict has ended.

Kriesberg endorses Coser's definition of conflict termination, but raises the problem of some parties, but not all, agreeing that the conflict has ended.

> Terminating a conflict means that some people agree that it has ended. Either partisans or observers assert that it has ended. Partisan definitions of conflict termination may be explicit or implicit and may be asserted by only one side or agreed upon by both. There is usually a symbolically important event or an explicit agreement in order for both sides to agree that a conflict

has ended. . . . Lacking such events, or simply not accepting
their significance, one side may refuse to agree that the struggle has ended. Obviously, this is generally the "defeated" side.
Its continuance, or renewal of conflict behavior, generally
forces the other side to do so also.

   History does not end. But that does not, and should not,
stop us from writing histories. We must accept the often arbitrary demarcations of conflict terminations, but we should be
explicit about the criteria used to mark the end of a conflict
(Kriesberg 1973).

In accordance with Coser and Kriesberg, we amend our definition of conflict termination by excising the notion that contending
parties will be satisfied. Rather, the contending parties merely
should agree that the issue has been resolved. Failing unanimous
agreement, we may have to designate arbitrary but explicit demarcations of conflict termination. Such definitions will be developed in
terms of the behavior of authoritative school district and city officials. Possible definitions include voting and nonvoting decisions by
legislative bodies, decisions by administrative personnel, and such
"nondecisions" as failure or refusal to place an issue on the agenda
of a formal meeting, or the cessation of demands by contending parties.

Coping with Conflict

   Mintzberg argues that the question of what managers do has
never been answered. His attempt, and especially his isolation of
the role of manager as "disturbance handler," is helpful. He main-
tains, however, without evidential support, that the management of
public or private enterprise is essentially the same (Mintzberg 1973,
p. 14).

   We argue that there are substantial differences. Private managers do not have representative functions, and are not responsible
for making authoritative value decisions, or managing social conflict. However, public managers and private managers *do* have to
manage conflict. Most writers begin discussion of conflict management with conflict termination, but since our definition of conflict
indicates an active component, we can begin a discussion of conflict
management from that point. While this equation is not completely

inaccurate, we prefer to argue that conflict management requires the resolution of conflict and the satisfaction of competitors' demands, at least to the extent that perceptions of goal incompatibility are not accompanied by perceptions of opportunity for blocking behavior. The cessation of conflictual activity, then, is our starting point. Conflict has been managed when the parties to the dispute abandon (albeit temporarily) active blocking behavior. Conflicts, then, are never necessarily "resolved"; they are merely made passive.

Social science literature, as typified, for example, by Banfield and Wilson (1963), asserts that conflict is best managed (converted from active to passive) by being regulated. As Dye and Hawkins put it: "Government regulates conflict by establishing and enforcing general rules by which conflict is to be carried on, by arranging compromises and balancing interests, and by imposing settlements which the parties to the disputes must accept" (1967, p. 8).

In school governance, municipal governance, and indeed all governance, this task is not necessarily easy. It is less difficult in systems with institutionalized channels of communications among elites and masses, and between elites (e.g., political parties and established interest groups). In the absence of institutionalized and legitimate conflict articulation, management becomes more complex. Indeed, some, such as Barnard (1958) believe that the natural, most instinctive response is not to regulate, but to *avoid* conflict by reducing contact between conflicting parties (Nebgen 1978), by preventing potential controversies from achieving formal agenda status (Cobb and Elder 1972), and by playing for time.

Intraorganizational conflict is occasionally resolved in this manner, especially when such conflicts are a consequence of misperception of conflicting individual goals. Conflict between subordinates, for example, may go away if it is based largely upon minor, noninstitutionalized interactions.

However, it seems clear that avoidance of social conflict can result in conflict expansion, first to articulate publics, and then perhaps to normally passive masses (Cobb and Elder 1972, p. 81). The literature on fluoridation and school desegregation strongly supports the notion that avoidance leads to increased lay participation. Increased lay participation leads to a more complex management problem, perhaps to the "ripple effect" whereby conflicts overlap and groups coalesce.

As we have written on numerous occasions, school managers apparently are more attuned to subordinate conflict management than to lateral or superordinate ones. When combined with the lack of institutional channels of access, the possibility exists of minor disputes becoming major ones.

Conflicts that escalate because of avoidance or procedural insensitivity are clearly amenable to various tracing strategies such as organizational development, as Golembiewski has argued (1965). Conflicts that are a consequence of the structure of a community (heterogeneity, population growth, etc.) are less easily managed. Successful politicians manage with a combination of persuasion, bargaining, negotiation, and compromise, strategies not included in the training of an expert, especially if the disputants are not perceived as belonging to the community of experts.

The norm of bargaining, the give and take of politics, is not, however, absent from conflict resolution. We have distinguished between bargaining among experts and bargaining between experts and lay persons (see also Peterson 1976). The two types are not, of course, mutually exclusive. Experts may seek the support of lay persons, especially community influentials or active groups. Indeed, one possible distinction between municipal and school governance is the extent to which such coalitions are built (see below).

Intraorganizational conflict, even though Bailey would classify most of it as subordinate, frequently involves bargaining among experts. Here, conflict management assumes the characteristics that normally concern students of organizations—the issues are likely to be only loosely anchored to strongly held ideological preferences and beliefs, and the expertise of bargainers is acknowledged and respected (see Gross et al., 1958). Management strategies are based upon these assumptions. They are generally described as "rational." Thus, according to Blake and Mouton (1961), the following activities constitute a process for conflict management: (1) definition of the problem; (2) review of the problem; (3) development of a range of alternatives; (4) reaching for solutions; (5) explanation and evaluation of solutions; (6) weighing alternative solutions; and (7) selection of the appropriate solutions.

Broader social and political conflict rarely is managed by using such a process. Under conditions of expanded or "rancorous" conflict, in Gamson's (1966) terminology, the conflicting individuals or groups are likely to attach strongly held ideologies to their goals and to be unwilling to acknowledge the legitimacy of expertise.

As conflict expands, the issues become more abstract and unclear; that is, less subject to easy identification. Specific problems are generalized, complex issues are distorted and simplified, and new conflicts develop as a subset of the original ones. This process is described by Coleman (1957) and Gamson (1968). Cobb and Elder, as noted, are also concerned with expanded conflict. The most systematic analysis is by Edelman. He noted that a common phenomenon in politics is that conflicts appear to be muted and conflicting groups satisfied without any discernible reallocation of tangible resources (Edelman 1964). He argued that this was the case because "it is characteristic of large numbers of people in our society that they see and think in terms of stereotypes, personalizations, and oversimplifications, that they cannot recognize or tolerate ambiguous and complex situations, and that they accordingly respond chiefly to symbols that oversimplify and distort" (p. 31). Subsequent research has supported Edelman's view (for a convenient summary, see Dye and Zeigler 1984).

Empirical examination of the implications of Edelman's work for conflict management occasionally considered the role of symbol manipulation in the achievement of acquiescence among protest groups (Lipsky 1970). While this line of inquiry could be pursued, we believe a more useful application is to place symbolic satisfaction squarely within our discussion of conflict management, a point not developed by Lipsky and other students of protest.

The broader the conflict—the more public and visible the arena—the less relevant to conflict management become the resources of the expert. The frustrations of experts at the inutility of rational argument is well illustrated by the fluoridation literature. For instance, water quality, an extraordinarily complex issue engaging the attention of highly trained professionals, is translated by the public into simplistic slogans such as "clean water versus jobs"— slogans that reduce the complexities of the issues to understandable terms.

Political leaders, whose resources are electoral, achieve success by symbol manipulation, especially by the introduction of sym-

bols denoting an enemy: George Wallace versus "pointy-headed intellectuals," Richard Nixon versus "bums," or Jimmy Carter versus
"greedy oil companies."

These kinds of symbols are, as noted, foreign to nonelected but
publicly accountable executives. In fact, such executives lack effective ways of responding to symbol manipulation. Hence, they seek
to avoid the expansion of conflict.

It is easier, Cobb and Elder believe, to prevent expansion than
to resolve expanded conflict. Their example of conflict expansion is
illustrative of the process described above.

> The conflict began as a dispute between a group of teachers and
> a local school board. The Teachers' Union . . . rallied to the sup-
> port of the teachers, calling their dismissal an issue on which all
> teachers must take a stand. Other municipal unions . . . rallied
> behind the Teachers' Union, since all workers have a stake in
> the dispute. As the conflict was expanded and was redefined,
> the issue of anti-semitism was raised. This brought the Jewish
> residents of New York City into the fray. They sided with the
> teachers only because of the larger issues involved. Of course,
> by this time the better informed strata of the general public had
> become aware of the conflict, which eventually filtered to the
> general public when the teachers went on strike (Rosenthal
> 1969, p. 154).

Conflict detection is an integral part of conflict management.
Cobb and Elder refer to this as *anticipation*. By anticipating that a
passive conflict may become active, it is possible to regulate its expansion. If this is done, managers maintain some control over the
agenda and the participants and hence, some influence over the resolution. If anticipation does not occur, management becomes more
reactive and utilizes the tools of reactive conflict management. Pre-
eminent among these are discrediting the goals, leadership, or motives of an antagonistic group; coopting group leaders into an institutional web, frequently by the creation of committees; and
providing symbolic reassurance by the same device. By such
means, argue Piven and Cloward, the Great Society programs "had
the effect of absorbing and directing many of the agitational elements in the black population" (1977, p. 276).

A less overt political strategy is to contain conflict by *individualizing* it. Managers, more than elected officials, have recourse to this method. Our own research, and that of Eisinger (1972) and of Katz, Gutek, Kahn, and Barton (1975) have shown that citizen-manager communications tend to concern the redress of individual grievances. School managers, we know, spend more time resolving individual complaints than answering requests or demands for policy decisions. The degree to which such complaints can be resolved without resorting to policy modification will be an important predictor of the extent to which conflict can be contained. If individual requests are treated responsively, collective action is less likely to take place.

These strategies, in a variety of combinations, are available for use in conflict management for the prevention or cessation of active blocking behavior. Our definition of conflict, then, leads to this conceptualization of conflict management behavior:

1. Conflict has been managed when the parties to the dispute abandon, or at least suspend, active blocking behavior. The management of conflict is the conversion of conflict from an active to a passive state.
2. Successful management institutionalizes conflict.
3. Social conflict is not managed by avoidance; on the contrary, avoidance leads to expansion and wider public participation and, consequently, to a more complex management problem.
4. Management of intraorganizational conflict involves a different set of activities than does the management of broader social and political conflict. In intraorganizational conflict, the issues are not likely to have a strong ideological component and the expertise of the parties is accepted. In expanded public conflicts, the parties are likely to attach strongly held ideologies to their goals and to be unwilling to acknowledge the legitimacy of expertise. Symbol manipulation, for example, is more appropriate for handling these conflicts than for resolving intraorganizational conflicts.
5. The management behaviors associated with the public conflicts we are interested in are directed toward controlling the expansion of conflict.

—3—

The Winnowing Process

Selection

To be a professional, whatever else you may do, you must get an education. Education does not necessarily make people better in their jobs; it merely certifies that they *should* be able to do the work. Obviously, the policy makers in a profession that dispenses education as a public good are expected to be highly educated. The ideological assumptions surrounding the creation of the superintendency, so well explained by Tyack (1974), were clearly in support of the notion that only the educated can educate; no further exposition was necessary. An expert must look and talk like one; in education, this means getting a doctorate.

Although the profession of city manager emerged at approximately the same time as the superintendency and was supported by similar ideologies, there is less stress upon credentials for that position. Whether this is the case because there is no "one best way" in municipal government, or because city governments traditionally have proved to be more permeable than school district governments, it is apparent that one can manage a city with less formal education than is required to manage a school district. In their heart of hearts, city managers may long for a sanitized, apolitical life, but they know their hopes are unrealistic. Superintendents have more of a stake in the idea that the delivery of their services is essentially technical. It is easy to argue (with some justification) that schooling is too complex and too delicate to be controlled by normal politics; it is harder to make that case for municipal politics.

Systems, such as schools, that stress the authority of expertise expect credentials. Superintendents can deliver. In our study 73 percent of the superintendents, as opposed to only 10 percent of the city managers, hold doctoral degrees. Two-thirds of the city managers did not continue beyond the master's degree, and 28 percent have earned only the bachelor's degree. *No* superintendent has only a bachelor's degree; those without the doctorate have at least a master's.

These findings are not surprising. There is a direct, unavoidable, career path to the superintendency. The primary avenue for getting ahead is to obtain a doctorate in education. Many districts stipulate this requirement in their job descriptions. Such requirements appear more pervasive over time. There is a fascinating "winnowing" process at work here. Although the issue is modestly clouded by the possibility of having a double major in undergraduate work, superintendents were more likely to major in education than any other subject. Thirty-six percent earned their undergraduate degrees in education; the remainder were scattered approximately evenly throughout the curricula of the undergraduate college. Of all superintendents who hold a master's degree only, 81 percent earned their degrees in education, and of those who hold doctoral degrees, 95 percent were completed in education. Clearly, specialization occurs early. Whatever the merits of a generalized education, they are lost on superintendents who choose to major in education early in their careers and stay with it until they have finished.

By contrast, city managers show less inclination to specialize early. Although there is no specialization for city managers directly comparable to education, public administration probably comes closest. Only 14 percent of city managers majored in public administration as undergraduates. Two-thirds were social science majors, and one-fourth graduated from business schools. While 70 percent were public administration majors in their master's level training, this percentage is still substantially lower than that of superintendents who major in education.

The evidence here is clear; the path to the superintendency is more narrow and specialized than is the path to the city manager's office. Whatever the merits of a generalized education, they are *not* lost on city managers. Of course much can be said for the demands of the market; if city governments required Ph.D.'s they would get them. But they do not, and this tells us something about the development of professional expectations. City councils apparently assume that cities can be managed by less formally educated people than is true for school districts. Further, people who become city managers spend their undergraduate years in relatively abstract, nonoccupational training. We all are familiar with the reputations of schools of education; they are generally held in low regard by those in other disciplines. They typically attract the students with the poorest records of achievement. This is not to say that all superintendents are ignorant. It probably is accurate to say, however, that their education was generally less challenging and less controversial than is true of city managers. It is certainly accurate to say that on average, their educational experience placed greater emphasis on deference to established authority.

Additionally, there is the increased probability of encountering a cohesive monopoly in ideology, one hallmark of a profession. Education schools not only are more distant intellectually from colleges of arts and sciences, they also are more clearly connected to a practicing profession—the superintendency. Schools of education, and especially the programs in educational administration, were created to supply the nation's schools with managers. With this kind of background, it is not surprising that education schools have more of an "applied" mentality. Education majors generally intend to get jobs in public schools. For graduate students in public administration, the career path is not so narrow: one may aspire to be a city manager, work for a state or local bureaucracy, seek federal employment, enter the private sector, and so on. While this is also the case in schools of education, here the superintendency is generally considered the plum.

Superintendents earn their graduate degrees *after* they have been employed (as a teacher perhaps) in public schools. The pressure to gain higher credentials drives aspiring teachers back to school for a master's degree or an equivalent number of credits in order to obtain a permanent certificate as a teacher. Usually at a later point would-be superintendents return to colleges of education in order to become credentialed as school administrators, hence interrupting their formal education several times. However, controlling for age, superintendents earn their undergraduate and graduate degrees earlier than do city managers.* Since there is no significant difference in age between city managers and superintendents, it is

*These differences in years are statistically significant differences at less than 0.5 level for a two-tailed T-test.

the city managers, not the superintendents, who pursue the greater mix of practical and ivory tower experience.

Still, everything points to the superintendents as a more professionally committed group. It is also probable that they have gone to a more prestigious university. Using a quality-ranking system developed by the Carnegie Council (Roizen et al. 1978), we examined the reputations of the universities from which superintendents and city managers received their highest degrees. This ranking system ranges from 1 (most prestigious) to 7 (least prestigious). Both city managers and superintendents have top-of-the-line degrees. The average rank for superintendents is 2.2 and that of city managers a modestly lower 2.5.

These modest, but consistent, differences describe superintendents as more highly educated and specialized than city managers. Superintendents make an earlier career choice and finish their educational training earlier.

Policy and Administration

To return to the tension between democracy and professionalism, the complexity of factors we associate with high professionalism can lead to managers or superintendents being more responsive to extra-local pressures than to local ones. A professional agenda can develop without much regard for the problem of responsiveness to local demands. The job of being locally responsive is that of the city council or school board.

This division of labor makes good sense; unfortunately it does not account for the growing tendency for expert knowledge to replace representative obligation as the "currency" of local politics. It is too much to ask of a professional that he or she refrain from imposing judgment upon the deliberations of the amateur legislatures of local politics. Except for the biggest cities, which do not have city managers, local elected office is a part-time occupation and staff service is minimal. When local amateurs are in the process of making wrong-headed decisions, what professional could resist setting them right?

Setting them right means getting involved in policy. We are all familiar with the policy/administration division of labor. Although largely discredited today, the assumption that politics and administration are separate has enjoyed wide currency in the literature of public administration. A legacy of the reform movement, the separation of policy and administration was given elegant expression by Woodrow Wilson in 1887 and Frank Goodnow in 1900 (Stillman 1973).

Recent reexamination of those writings suggests that they were misinterpreted, but no matter. The U.S. science of public administration was built on the notion of neutral competence. The political and administrative functions of government are separable. Administration should not be concerned with political expediency or partisan concerns. Actually, Wilson was an empiricist before his time and it is likely that he really meant that administration should only be separate from partisan and patronage politics, those characteristics of the urban machines he sought to eliminate. That he meant administrators should not bargain, compromise, build coalitions, and lobby is doubtful (Stillman 1973).

Much of the support for separation of policy from administration was spawned by the scientific management ideology accompanying reform. But our evidence suggests that educational governance accepted the ideology of reform more completely than did municipal governance. Thompson argues that there is, indeed, an educational "ideology" (a systematic statement of beliefs), which lends itself more readily to the blandishments of scientific management:

> Educators have been notably successful in developing and conveying to others a set of ideological doctrines indicating that education is a unique governmental service that must be "kept out of politics". These beliefs have given them considerable autonomy and insulation from public pressures. As a result, the policy-making processes in school districts differ from the policy-making processes in other local governmental units (Thompson 1976, p. 46).

Our data certainly support this view. Superintendents buy the ideology far more than do city managers. Consequently, one could well argue that a contrasting ideology of education that stresses the desirability of "localism" is violated. There is a strain of schizophrenia running through school governance. As Thompson suggests, the educational bureaucracy is more unyielding than other local bureaucracies in its claim for the superiority of scientific, professional management over the representative legitimacy of lay boards. Yet there are lay boards, and there is the belief in "localism." School government is localism *in extremis*. Since the education of youth is more important than other services normally provided at the local level, and since the delivery of education to its clients requires more skill, training, and knowledge than is true of the delivery of other local services, schools have been given a unique institutional arrangement—the independent school district.

The tension between appointed experts and lay legislatures is a natural consequence of the reformed zeal for efficiency. Much of the reform movement was inspired by a distaste for urban machines, the symbols of corruption and inefficiency. The reforms were undertaken, at least overtly, to eliminate the influence of machine bosses, and return local educational and municipal government to "the people." But the substitution of experts for bosses is an exchange that, ironically for those who argue that "grass roots" democracy is well served by the units of government physically closest to the client, is at odds with the principles of government and participation outlined by the framers of the U.S. Constitution.

Madison and his colleagues " . . . placed their faith in periodic elections, legislatures, and an elected chief executive rather than in a bureaucracy, however pure and efficient. There is nothing to suggest that they believed sound administration could compensate for bad political decisions. Redressing grievances and bad political decisions was the function of the political process, rather than of administrative machinery" (Page 1971, p. 15). Although writing at a time when modern bureaucracies were unknown, surely the framers of the Constitution would have been appalled at an ideology that places responsibility for the accountability of bureaucracies in elected bodies. Indeed, the obsession of Madison with separation of powers can be seen as a deliberate trade-off: less efficiency for more responsiveness. Concentrated political or governmental power was an evil that those who constructed the Constitution sought to avoid, even if they had to give up some efficiency. Dispersion of authority, distrust of bureaucracy, and faith in the political process are values not widely held among administrators.

The policy process begins with the development of a proposal. On this point both managers and superintendents agree: they should develop agendas and proposals for their amateur legislatures. Indeed, they are expected to do so. Still, superintendents do more recommending than city managers. Their job descriptions require them to be leaders, and as we have seen, they are willing to play the role. The superintendent, as a symbol of governance, is likely to be more active than the city manager in recommending courses of ac-

tion. In at least two-thirds of the cases in which a board vote is required, the superintendent's recommendation is communicated either in writing or informally (Tucker and Zeigler 1980). Board
members routinely report that most of the information they receive
about schools comes from the central office.

In some cases recommendations are clear and unequivocal.
The agenda will contain a problem to be resolved and the recommendation of the superintendent as to which alternative is preferred
and why. In other cases, the recommendation is less obvious. The
problem will be defined and several courses of action (each with advantages and disadvantages) will be outlined. Whether or not a
superintendent includes only a single recommendation or several is
largely a consequence of the degree of intra-staff consensus. If the
central office staff is united, there will generally be only one recommendation. If there are several opinions, the factionalism is reflected in the material transmitted to the board. However, when the
board is confronted with several courses of action it invariably will
ask the superintendent for a personal recommendation. Even if the
superintendent's recommendation is offensive to the staff, the extent of disagreement will not be known to the board.

Educational bureaucracies realize the political value of information and are reluctant to dissipate it.

> Experts deal in a scarce commodity: knowledge, which includes
> not only the knowledge to which they have access, i.e. their ex-
> pertise, but more importantly, the information they obtain and
> generate. Even if a prince defines his experts' mandates very
> narrowly and delegates no authority to them, he still allows
> them to gather facts. Experts always have the right to seek in-
> formation that is relevant to the problems they study. . . . Since
> information and knowledge bring power, all bureaucracies are
> anxious to conserve theirs. . . . Experts are aware that they
> cannot disagree among themselves if they want the prince
> and others to listen (Benveniste 1977, p. 24).

Sources of Information

Clear comparisons between boards of education and more overtly
legislative bodies come readily to mind. If legislatures are to legis-
late, they need information. It is true that most policy initiation has
shifted to executives. Mayors, city managers, governors, presi-
dents, and executive bureaucracies generally initiate policy and leg-

islatures react. It is not true, however, that most legislatures are as
consensually supportive as are school boards. Again, this suggests
that school boards, as institutions of legislative action, are lacking in
their open examination of differing viewpoints. Even as passive re-
cipients of policy initiated by executive bureaucracies, most legislatures develop some degree of specialization, especially if, as is normally the case, committees have access to staff resources
independent of the executive branch. Additionally, committees can,
while digesting executive recommendations, develop modifications
based upon the testimony of interest groups. Interest groups function most extensively at the level of committee hearings because
committees devote a substantial portion of their attention to the single policy of greatest interest to the affected groups. Groups are especially attuned to the composition of key committees, and expend
substantial resources in establishing informal communications with
committee members. Standing committee staffs also interact with
interest groups, in some cases virtually forming a policy network.

Such is not the case with school boards. Even in the 51 largest
boards in the country, fewer than half have standing committees,
and very few have independent staffs (National School Boards Association 1975). The structure then leads to consensus. Our data
show that standing committees are significantly less common in educational governance compared to municipal governance. It is true
that boards make some use of ad hoc committees, but such committees cannot duplicate the information gathering and group bargaining functions of standing committees. The institutionalization of
group interaction is lacking. An especially apt comparison between
a standing committee and the ad hoc committees frequently created
in school districts is in their compositions. Standing committees
consist of legislators, informed by a staff, in regular communication
with influential interest groups. Ad hoc committees, as used by
school districts, use *selected* interest groups and individuals. Those
selected become part of the actual committee and do not serve as
protagonists. Such committees become essential ingredients in
guaranteeing their cooptation. The values of such citizens ultimately come to reflect those of the board and the administration.
Such participation is not comparable to the participation of organized interest groups.

The absence of standing committees also contributes to the inability of boards to develop competing policy options. Administrators enjoy a substantial advantage in regular, sustained communica-

tion with other professionals. Walker (1971) has called attention to the dominance of a "horizontal" mode of communication in policy development. By rapidly spreading knowledge of new programs through meetings, seminars, and publications, and by contributing to the mobility of high-level administrators, professional associations help to shape consensus in policy areas concerning desirable programs and to indirectly influence policy agendas in state and local governments (Tucker and Zeigler 1980).

In an article entitled "Care and Feeding of Interest Groups: Interest Groups as Seen by a City School Superintendent," Donald Steele et al. (1981) point out that if an interest group is given the status of a standing committee then it is one which is selected by the district as "deserving" of a long-term commitment. In the same article Steele et al. point out that interest groups "can defuse the potency of competing interest groups" and "can have greater influence on the public than the most articulate of school administrators" (1981, p. 262). Hence, even where school districts do have standing committees they may be used by the superintendent to defuse groups in opposition or as a mouthpiece for the administration, rather than providing for greater lay participation in educational policy making.

As administrators are full-time professionals, their associations are stronger in providing opportunities for such horizontal communication than is the National School Boards Association. It is difficult, if not impossible, for board members to become experts. The absence of functional expertise is obvious in the way that boards conduct their business. One striking aspect of board decision making is the extent to which decisions are made. Although it may appear initially as a trivial point, the absence of a well-established committee structure and the relative quiescence of organized groups in any deliberations prior to public meetings indicate that boards can reach closure when they so desire. Compared with other legislative bodies, school boards do not become bogged down in the tedious process of compromise.

Votes of Confidence

All of this means that school boards should be less likely to reject the recommendations of superintendents than city councils are to reject the recommendations of city managers. This is true.

Table 3.1   Relationship Between Rejected Recommendations and Occupation, Controlling for Professional Attitudes

	Professional Attitude			
	Low		High	
No. Rejected Recommendations	Occupation			
	Superintendent	City Manager	Superintendent	City Manager
0–3	93%	33%	69%	50%
4 or more	7%	68%	31%	50%
	100%	101%*	100%	100%
	(16)	(30)	(35)	(22)

*Exceeds 100% due to rounding.

Among both the high and low professional categories, superintendents' proposals are rejected less frequently than are those of city managers. Given the deference to expertise characteristic of school districts, the greater success of superintendents is not astonishing. It is instructive here to recall the notion of the "beleaguered superintendent, browbeaten by once subservient boards of education" (Maeroff 1975). Superintendents probably think they *are* browbeaten, since they regard any defeat as a threat to professionalism. But they do better than city managers; indeed, city managers are browbeaten. At least half of them report having recommendations rejected four times in the previous year. Yet there is almost no literature on the "beleaguered city manager." Since they are less obsessed with winning, city managers probably regard losing a few now and again as normal.

The fact that school boards are more compliant than city councils is not the most significant aspect of this table. Of more interest is the relationship between professionalism and legislative success, which seems to work in opposite ways for city managers and superintendents. Highly professional superintendents *lose more* frequently than do less professional ones; highly professional city managers *lose less* frequently than do less professional ones.

What can we make of the irony that superintendents who expect the most deference get the least? City managers who expect the least get the most. Several explanations come to mind. It may be that highly professional superintendents have a narrow zone of tolerance. For them, a rejection may amount to anything less than blind obedience. Alternatively, they may lose more because they wish to avoid compromise even if failure to compromise will result in defeat. Both explanations are consistent with our theories of professionalism, and both are true to some extent. They will be discussed more carefully later in the book when we explain different modes of conflict management behavior. In the meantime, the fact that professionalism is correlated with a less compliant board is of profound import. Since schools of education are still producing experts, the fruits of their labor include, apparently, boards that increasingly compete with the superintendent for power.

This may be serious, indeed. For superintendents have a clear expectation, not apparently shared by city managers, that a vote against the administrative position is a vote of no confidence. Superintendents believe that there are two options available to a board: to trust them or to fire them. Compromise, in which the administrator adjusts his or her recommendations or perhaps abandons the less acceptable ones, is not considered "professional" to superintendents. As one text observes:

> A board has authority, of course, to formulate policies and pass motions to give policies effect on their own initiative, bypassing the superintendent. This should occur only rarely . . . when it occurs frequently the lack of rapport between the board and the superintendent and the misunderstanding of respective spheres calls for a drastic remedy in the form of replacing the superintendent, changing the board, or both. . . . Occasionally, the board will disagree with the superintendent's recommendation and act contrary to it. If this occurs more than occasionally, it indicates a lack of understanding between the board and superintendent . . . the superintendent must have the wholehearted support of the board. When he is no longer deserving of such support, it is time for a change in administration (Greider et al. 1961, pp. 131–43).

If one asks the average superintendent to define an "acceptable" rate of loss, rarely will he accept less than 95 percent. That is, if he "loses" more than 5 percent of his recommendations, he believes he should seek other employment. Whether or not he does, the "trust me or fire me" notion does not provide much opportunity for negotiation, especially as public school board meetings are largely devoid of public participation.

Professionalism and Career Patterns

Certainly we do not assume that education and professional commitment are prerequisites for "good" management. Indeed, just the opposite may be the case. When professionals confront situations in which professional expertise is of no value, what do they do? To compromise may run counter to their professional training but may be politically necessary. Professionals held accountable to elected lay persons may find it unbearably frustrating. If there is a profession, there must be professional knowledge. Such knowledge is the exclusive property of those who have earned the professional credentials: the "right" to profess. Therefore, superintendents may be unwilling to yield to the lay board regarding, for example, curricular decisions.

This all depends on whether schools of education do, in fact, graduate people who believe themselves to be professionals. Does the socialization process work? Strictly speaking, a professional is somebody who is paid to do what he or she does. But this is not what concerns us here. What we do care about is the sense of autonomy that is the essence of professionalism. Autonomy—freedom from constraint—is a demanding criterion for public officials accountable to city councils and school boards.

Professionalism and autonomy are nearly synonymous. Expert knowledge is the domain of the professional. Those who identify themselves, or are identified by others, as professionals are said to have a specialized competence which can be gained only through formal training. A natural consequence, of professionalization and the presumed acquisition of expert knowledge is the desire for autonomy.

> Having special knowledge at his command, the professional worker needs and seeks a large degree of autonomy from lay control and normal organizational control. Who is the best judge of surgical procedure—laymen, hospital administrators, or surgeons? Who is the best judge of theories in chemistry—laymen, university administrators, or professors of chemistry? As work becomes professionalized—specialized around esoteric knowledge and techniques—the organization must create room for expert judgment, and autonomy of decision-making and professional (Clark 1966, pp. 285–86).

Given its emphasis upon autonomy, the ideology of professionalism conflicts with proponents of lay control, grass roots democracy, or any mode of thinking that challenges autonomy. If city managers and superintendents regard themselves as experts, then they must achieve autonomy; failure to do so is to concede lack of expertise. More importantly, failure to achieve autonomy is to subvert expert knowledge, an exercise regarded by the putative holders of such knowledge as a betrayal of their profession.

As it turns out, these problems seem to be more severe for superintendents than for city managers, because they believe themselves to be more professional. Using Hall's Professional Attitude Scale as a measure, superintendents are far more inclined toward belief in professional autonomy (see Table 3.2).* For them, autonomy is fundamental; for city managers, autonomy is, while certainly not irrelevant, hardly an obsession.

Table 3.2   Level of Professional Commitment by Occupation

	Supts.	*C.M.*	
Low	35%	65%	N = 46
High	61%	39%	N = 57
		Total	N = 101

As directors of governments providing multiple services, city managers are more broadly educated than superintendents, and have less claim to expert certification (they typically do not have a doctorate). If your pothole is not filled up you can complain. If your child cannot read, what can you do? Either your pothole is fixed, or it is not. But your child cannot read because of a bewildering, complex, and frequently misunderstood combination of circumstances. Indeed, it is quite likely that there is nothing the school can do.

If the technology is "soft," its defense is not. Behind the claims of the superintendent for professional autonomy lies the weight of

---

*Each of the responses to the Professional Attitude Scale Items were ranked from 1 to 5 in order to provide a degree of agreement with the percepts associated with professionalism. Cumulative scores for each respondent provide the basis for a sample mean score. This mean score, which is 3.5, distinguished between low and high degrees of professionalism. The standardized Cronbach alpha reliability coefficient for this scale is .62, a conventionally accepted coefficient value (Henerson et al. 1978).

the schools of education. The professional networks in education are strong and educators seem to protect each other. Consider the following:

> Because the technology employed by school personnel is relatively imprecise. . . . Schools are more vulnerable to external shifts and faddism. In the face of this situation, it may be wise to protect the basic curriculum or technology of schools from frequent shifts in policy and program. In short, a preeminent requirement of school organizations as opposed to city councils may be to maintain the organization. Hence, boards, teachers, and administrators favor buffering the schools from the environment (Moore 1980a, p. 14).

It is reasonably safe to assert that in nominally democratic societies such as ours, one does not expect to hear a serious argument contending that elected representatives should shield policy making from the public. This could only happen in the field of education.

Thus the professionalism of superintendents exceeds that of city managers because of both the existence of a confirming ideology and a narrow career path. But how does one prevent slippage and keep the ideology reinforced? Professional associations can do this, if professionals can be persuaded to join them. Virtually all managers and superintendents belong to their respective associations, the International City Managers Association and the American Association of School Administrators.

Beyond these two major organizations, there are hundreds of regional and state associations, and an equal number of more specialized national ones. Organizational membership is an indicator of professionalism because it fosters "horizontal" modes of communication. Organizations facilitate intraprofessional communication and reinforce professional identification through meetings, workshops, and newsletters. By fostering occupational networks, they assist in the movement or transfer of professional personnel. These associations also help to develop and maintain policy consensus among professionals by rapidly spreading knowledge of new programs, ideas, or methodologies. Most superintendents are joiners— 80 percent belong to three or more organizations. City managers join fewer organizations; 58 percent belong to three or more organizations. Taken with their scores on the professionalism index, it is apparent that superintendents are more professional in training, attitude, and organizational reinforcement.

Ask school administrators to estimate how long the average tenure of a superintendent is and you will be told some horror stories. The kamikaze image of superintendents is one of the great myths of the 1980s. Beleaguered superintendents stand bravely before once subservient boards, refuse to compromise their professional standards, and are fired. The code phrase is "superintendents' burnout." As one superintendent stated, "About the only person whose job is less secure than an urban superintendent's is the manager of the New York Yankees. . . . It's not surprising that big city school superintendents end up getting fired with alarming regularity." Why so? Because "a superintendent has to take on battles or turn into a jellyfish. If that happens, then the kids go down the drain." Now that the stakes are defined—it's the kids—small wonder that the superintendent must be able to "look anyone in the face and say, 'Morally, I did what I thought I had to do.' " The solution is, of course, that the board must decide "to trust the superintendent or fire him" (Ficklen 1983, p. 19).

These accounts sound more like the memoirs of front-line commanders in Viet Nam than descriptions of the superintendency. And, fortunately, they are not accurate descriptions of the population of school superintendents, either for our sample or for the national sample surveyed recently by AASA (1982). Superintendents enjoy an average job tenure of just under eight years. City managers, who never find themselves the subject of articles about burnout, have a slightly shorter tenure of seven years. Additionally, managers normally operate without the contractual guarantees enjoyed by superintendents. Firing is less expensive because a reasonable notice is all that is required, hence no buying out of contracts.

Rather than being forced to compromise professional values or leave their respective professions altogether, city managers and superintendents move on and move up. Like any executive, public or private, they are ambitious. We traced the career patterns of individuals in both groups back to their three positions just preceding the present one. Individuals in both groups demonstrate the same patterns of mobility. The average number of years in the last job prior to the one currently held was five years for superintendents

Table 3.3 Type of Change and Duration in Administrative Career Patterns

	Position 1			Position 2			Position 3			Current Position			All Administrative Positions		
	Supt	C.M.	Sample	Supt	C.M.	Sample	Supt	C.M.	Sample	Supt	C.M.	Sample	Supt	C.M.	Sample
CHANGE															
Mean	4.27	3.50	3.98	4.14	3.73	3.95	4.00	3.79	3.90						
Mode	5	4	4	5	4	4	4	4	4						
SD	.77	.96	.92	.87	.90	.90	.78	.95	.87						
Sample	37	22	59	42	37	79	50	42	92						
DURATION															
Mean	4.35	3.27	3.95	4.60	3.49	4.08	5.14	5.14	5.14	7.73	7.06	7.39	20.63	18.75	19.68
Mode	2	4	4	2	3	3	3	3	3	6	1	1	15	10	20
SD	2.99	2.59	2.87	2.73	1.97	2.45	3.69	3.51	3.59	6.28	5.89	6.06	6.46	8.40	7.52
Range (in years)	1–13	1–13	1–13	1–12	1–7	1–12	1–17	1–20	1–20	1–28	1–27	1–28	6–35	1–35	1–35
Sample	37	22	59	42	37	79	50	42	92	51	52	103	51	52	103

#1 = Big step down
2 = Moderate step down
3 = About the same
4 = Moderate step up
5 = Big step up

and city managers. Prior to this, city managers moved more frequently. In both their first and second jobs, city managers had shorter tenure than did superintendents.

As they move on, there is a modest tendency to slow down. Superintendents and city managers tend to stay the longest in their third jobs, probably because by the time they have held two jobs with increased salaries, the market for their services is somewhat constricted.

Moving on is not necessarily moving up. By examining the size of the city or school district, the salary, and the individual's own opinion, we devised a scale based on the type of position and the size of the district (municipality) to estimate whether each move was a big step down, a moderate step down, a lateral move, a moderate step up, or a big step up. On a scale of 1 to 5 (1 signifying a big step down; 5 signifying a big step up), superintendents are more upwardly mobile than are city managers. Superintendents move up when they move out. For all three jobs prior to the present one, the mean is 4 or above. This is less true for city managers. All three of their previous jobs registered somewhere between a lateral move and a moderate step up. One explanation is the smaller market for city managers. There are nearly 16,000 school districts requiring a superintendent, but there are only about 2,000 municipalities that employ managers. The vast majority of these municipalities are small (under 25,000). However, there is a curious aspect to the mobility data. Whereas the superintendents have an upwardly mobile pattern on the whole, each successive move is slightly *less* prestigious. For city managers, mobility is less progressive in the aggregate, but each successive move is a modest step up. A city manager may have entered his or her present job from a variety of positions: city manager of another city, assistant city manager, planner, or even a private sector management position. Superintendents operate more within a well-defined hierarchy—moving from teacher, to principal, to assistant superintendent, to superintendent. The closer the potential superintendent gets to the ultimate prize, the less opportunity there is for upward mobility.

Mobility is often used to assess professionalism. As described earlier, administrators are regarded as "professionally oriented" or "bureaucratically oriented" (Scott 1966); "career bound" or "place bound" (Carlson 1962), or "cosmopolitan" or "local" (Gouldner 1954). The common theme of all these labels is the effort to distinguish between administrators who are motivated by professionally derived standards and those who are more responsive to their employing organization. Like us, these authors are groping for the essence of professionalism, autonomy, responsiveness to abstract professional standards, and interaction with colleagues remote from the place of employment. Professionally driven administrators will be restless, seeking new challenges. Locally responsive administrators will be content to stay put.

A more detailed analysis of career patterns leads us to offer a modification of the traditional two-part classification. Our categories include: movers and shakers, movers, slow progressors, and roller coasters. The first two categories are the most professional. These people are characterized by rapid movement (above average) from one position to the next. Movers and shakers move up consistently, while movers do not. The slow progressors are the bureaucratically oriented administrators. At least one previous position was above average in duration, and each change was at least a lateral one. Roller coasters display no consistent pattern, either in duration or direction of their mobility.

Our administrators are fairly evenly distributed among the two professionally oriented categories and the bureaucratically oriented category. Given what we have learned so far, we would suspect that the superintendents are more professional in career patterns. Although there are a few more movers and shakers among superintendents, there are more movers among city managers. Most importantly, half of the superintendents, the "locals," are slow progressors. Only one-third of the city managers are classified as slow progressors. Were it not for the fact that there are more roller coasters among city managers, we would have no trouble in concluding that while superintendents talk like professionals, they behave like locals, city managers talk like locals but they move along like professionals. The roller coaster pattern reflects the less rigid hierarchy constraining mobility in city government. One can move up, down, in, and out. This is less true for superintendents. This difference is only one of many that will appear as we explore other ways of comparing managers and superintendents. One possible explanation for these findings may stem from the fact that superintendents generally have contracts whereas city managers generally do not have that degree of job security. Therefore, city managers may be more likely to make a move that may not necessarily be considered to be upwardly mobile, thereby falling into the categories of "mover" and "roller coaster," rather than face the risk of temporary unemployment (which would act to their detriment in the job-search process).

Table 3.4   Crosstabulation Between Administrative Career Mobility Pattern and Occupation

	Occupation	
Pattern	Superintendent	City Manager
Mover and Shaker	24% (12)	19% (8)
Mover	18% (9)	29% (12)
Slow Progressor	50% (25)	33% (14)
Roller Coaster	8% (4)	19% (8)
	100% (50)	100% (42)

Leadership Orientation and Authority

The response of school districts to the uneasy relationship between experts and lay legislatures has been to concentrate authority in the office of the superintendent. Superintendents are *not* expected to be neutral. A glance at the handbooks prepared for school boards (there are no comparable documents for city councils) is instructive. Such handbooks are explicit about *half* of the policy-administration division of responsibility:

> It is agreed by authorities in the field of educational administration that the legislation of policies is the most important function of the school board and that the execution of these policies should be left wholly to the professional expert. Boards of education do not have the time to execute policies nor do they have the technical training needed for such work. In summary, the function of the board of education is not to run the schools but to see that they are run effectively.

Rarely, however, are boards cautioned about the reverse situation—the introduction of the superintendent into policy making. In fact, they are urged to expect that superintendents will initiate policy recommendations:

> It is often said that the board makes policy and the superintendent administers it. This is not the way in which effective boards operate. In actual practice the superintendent generally initiates policy-making and provides evidence on which the board makes decisions.

So much for the legacy of reform. The tension between professionals and amateurs is resolved by concentrating authority. Quotes

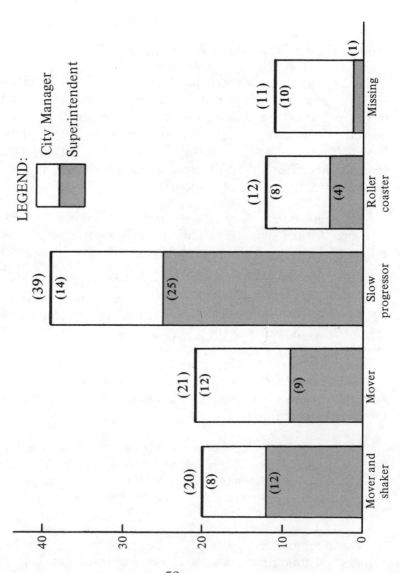

Chart 1 Histogram of Administrative Career Mobility Patterns

LEGEND:
City Manager
Superintendent

from the texts in educational administration, presumably encountered by fledgling superintendents, endlessly proclaim this theme:

> The board must rely for leadership on its chief executive officer, the superintendent . . . the board may be regarded in much the same light as a board of directors of a business corporation and the superintendent as the president or general manager in immediate charge of operation. . . . Legislation must be guided by what administration knows about schools . . . a superintendent may be expected to be somewhat in advance of the board's thinking because of his special interest and preparation. It is perfectly correct for him to participate in policy-making because of his special knowledge and preparation . . . (Greider et al. 1961, pp. 113–43).

Thus, the superintendent is expected to carry out three major responsibilities. First, the superintendent sets the agenda. About 75 percent of agenda items are placed there by the superintendent or a member of the central office staff (Tucker and Zeigler 1980, p. 124). Second, the superintendent makes executive recommendations. In fact, two-thirds of all agenda items are supported by such recommendations (Tucker and Zeigler 1980, p. 144). Third, the superintendent implements and evaluates policy.

Superintendents cannot be neutral experts who only follow orders. Indeed, superintendents, far more than city managers, characterize their jobs as providing strong leadership, that is, making policy. Leadership orientation can be measured by an eight-item scale, including such items as advocating major change in policies, helping the election of "good" school board members or city council members, and selling programs to the community.* The results of our evaluation of leadership orientation reveal a clear difference between superintendents and city managers. Superintendents believe they should be leaders; city managers see themselves more as neutral experts (see Table 3.5).

---

*The responses to the leadership scale items were ranked from 1 to 4, according to the degree of leadership. Cumulative scores for the complete scale were divided at the same mean to distinguish between low and high leadership roles. The standardized Cronbach alpha reliability coefficient for this scale is .64.

Influencing Elections

Curiously, superintendents are more likely to advocate involvement in the election and reelection of sympathetic board members than are city managers. Specifically regarding involvement in the electoral process, the statements to which superintendents responded in significantly higher levels of agreement, compared to city managers, were:

> A superintendent (city manager) should give a helping hand to good board (council) members seeking election, and a superintendent (city manager) should encourage people whom he/she respects to run for the school board (city council).

While a previous survey of board members has shown that professional school personnel (14 percent) and board members already in office (29 percent) often were the primary source of encouragement to run for the school board (Zeigler, Jennings, and Peak 1974, p. 34), this is the first time comparative data have been available.

Overt efforts to manipulate elections would seem to be beyond the boundaries of even the most liberally defined leadership role. Obviously, superintendents want boards that understand who does what; hence it is to their advantage to make sure that board members know something about school governance. Yet is such behavior "professional"? It is entirely reasonable to suppose that superintendents with strong professional values would *not* want to tarnish their apolitical images. But school board elections are hardly of the rough and tumble variety. Most incumbents are not challenged, most campaigns emphasize innocuous clichés (the best education for the least money), and turnout is (understandably) low. So superintendents can attempt to influence board elections without getting dirty. Municipal elections, while hardly models of party competition, are somewhat more issue oriented. City managers may decide to lay low since they are not authority figures.

In the same survey, superintendents advocated a stronger stance in policy making than did city managers (see Table 3.5). Superintendents generally approved the following statement: A superintendent should advocate major changes in school policies, and a superintendent should advocate policies to which important parts of the community may be hostile. These results give additional evidence to support the arguments that superintendents, in fact, domi-

Table 3.5 Leadership Role and Occupation

	Occupation			
	School Superintendent		City Manager	
Leadership Role				
Low	37%	(20)	63%	(34)
High	63%	(31)	37%	(18)
	100%	(51)	100%	(52)

nate educational policy making. Perhaps the reason that superintendents spend less time overall managing conflict than do city
managers is that they have so much control over the educational
policy-making arena that conflicts are much less apt to arise.

Still, the notion that politics and administration can be sepa-
rated is a theory without much support among current students of
public administration. Traditionally captive to the scientific management school, the field of public administration gained new respect when it admitted the futility of any real world separation of
politics and administration. Woodrow Wilson himself probably
never took the separation of politics and administration as seriously
as did his followers. Although there were many debunkers, authors
of essays in Fritz Morstein-Marx's *Elements of Public Administration* (1946) set the tone. Most of the authors in this volume were
academics who had administrative experience during and after
World War II. They described administration as highly politicized,
with bureaucrats scrambling for power and money just like every-
one else. In any case, it is not viewed as unprofessional for managers
and superintendents to propose policy. Indeed, certainly in the case
of school superintendents, policy proposal is expected. Evidence
that city managers are expected to initiate policy also exists, although we discovered them far less inclined to do so.

City managers may be less dominant policy makers because
their legislatures are more active. Loveridge points to "positional
differences" in municipal governance. He argues that because of recruitment and socialization, the manager's self-image is one of policy maker. Managers want to be active participants in city governments, not paper shufflers. In Loveridge's words:

> Most managers have a cosmopolitan outlook focused primarily
> on a set of professional standards. These values are accen-

tuated by detailed information, staff pressures, awareness of
problems—local and national—and short tenure (Loveridge
1971, p. 98).

So far managers sound like superintendents. But what of city
councils? Councils believe managers to be "well-paid employee[s],
expected to give unrequited loyalty to the city, to be governed by the
directives of the council, and to accept the policy hopes and goals
of councilmen—'city managers should be on top' " (Loveridge
1971). Loveridge hastens to add that, in fact, managers have no
choice but to become active in policy making.

Still, the differences between city councils and school boards
are striking. School boards do not expect to govern superintendents
with their directives; rather the boards expect to be governed in
their public behavior by the preferences of the superintendent. Although the current ideology of educational administration argues
that superintendents are "browbeaten by once subservient boards"
(Maeroff 1975) the evidence belies this contention. Superintendents
set agendas, make policy recommendations, and almost never lose.
Board votes normally are unanimous and support the policies of the
superintendent. There is no evidence to suggest that school boards
are even remotely as active in policy making as city councils, as will
be described more thoroughly in the next chapter. The conflict described by Loveridge as troublesome for city managers does not exist (except in rare cases) for superintendents.

Hence, superintendents are more policy active because they
are expected to be. They develop a strong proprietary feeling about
the shape of the educational program. They believe that this program should not be the province of elected boards because boards
are technically uninformed and may make decisions that are harm-
ful to "the kids" (almost everything that superintendents do can be
rationalized by the statement that they were doing "what's best for
the kids"). One superintendent had an especially elegant way of describing his policy-action behavior: "I want the board to understand
as much as they possibly can, but I don't want to overload them.
Sometimes they think they have to take a position on these issues if I
discuss them with them. But instructional matters go over their
heads." Another superintendent defines his "turf" as "anything
that has to do with programs." By programs he means "curriculum,
textbook selection, placement of teachers and principals, personnel

recommendations." Yet another explains that he believes in discussing all policy areas openly with "his" board, but only for show: "I consult and inform the board, but this doesn't change the direction I am headed . . . but the board feels better about it."

The city managers, in spite of the professional commitment described by Loveridge, do not claim such autonomy. One, recalling the "Woodrow Wilson theory" of his school years, concedes that the council involves itself in administrative matters: "The council gets elected on issues that involve city departments because they believe that's where the action is." Such meddling would cause a superintendent to demand, and get, a vote of confidence and a promise to leave him alone. For city managers, council involvement in administration is a fact of life: "On planning and goals I want input, but they are the boss." Out of the same reform tradition emerge two different views of administration: one professional, the other perhaps "semi-professional."

Bureaucratic Leadership

Leadership is not, as is normally assumed, charismatic, or even political; it is technical. In his profound study of leadership, James McGregor Burns explains what is meant by bureaucratic leadership: "It (bureaucracy) is a world that prizes consistency, predictability, stability, and efficiency (narrowly defined) more than creativity and principle." Burns then makes the startling assertion that "bureaucratic behavior as characterized in this archetype is antithetical to leadership as defined in this volume" (Burns 1978, p. 296). Indeed it is. Burns, speaking for the discipline of political science, defines leadership as occurring *"when persons with certain motives and purposes mobilize, in competition or conflict with others, institutional, political, psychological, and other resources so as to arouse, engage, and satisfy the motives of followers"* (1978, p. 18; emphasis added).

It is unlikely that superintendents and city managers will achieve the stage of leadership ability as defined by Burns, but they still can be leaders of the bureaucratic variety. Rather than mobilizing followers, they mobilize information. If controversy is to be avoided, the information is phrased so that all win. How one views leadership, however, is not solely defined by immediate circum-

**Table 3.6   Relationship Between Leadership Role and
Occupation, Controlling for Professional Attitude**

	Professional Attitude			
	Low		High	
	Occupation			
Leadership Role	Superintendent	City Manager	Superintendent	City Manager
Low	38%	60%	40%	73%
High	63%	40%	60%	27%
	101%*	100%	100%	100%
	(16)	(30)	(35)	(22)

*Exceeds 100 due to rounding.

stance. People trained to rely upon information, in all likelihood, will be attracted to a technocratic-analytic mode of rational problem solving, while those less ideologically committed will find the Burns definition acceptable.

To behave in the Burns mode, meaning to utilize motivational techniques, does not mean that one adopts a raving, anti-intellectual populism. George Wallace need not be the model. To mobilize coalitions, according to Burns, merely requires that managers be willing to bargain compromise a bit, and lobby for their professional beliefs. If the technocratic leadership mode is "rational," then the political one is merely "non-rational" (not "irrational").

Much of the reaction in public administration to the extreme scientism of the reform movement has been in the direction of modifying excessive reliance upon rational modes of conflict resolution. Although it is difficult to imagine now, Herbert Simon's *Administrative Behavior* (1947) became a major challenge to scientific management. Simon's rigorously scientific approach to the *study* of administration has led many to assume wrongly that he wants managers to manage conflict by the numbers. Other social scientists have emphasized the futility, even the danger, of managing with scientific axioms rather than with a sure knowledge of the political terrain.

It is well they might write in this mode, for the relationship between professionalism and leadership is far from clear. The leadership scale decidedly leans toward the political end of the spectrum (see Appendix B). This scale addresses a chief executive's initiative in advocating policy change, the degree to which a stand is taken on controversial issues and activity in legislative elections. These are obviously measures of political leadership.

Theoretically, people who are strongly professional should eschew political leadership. This conclusion is not supported by the data. Again, one would expect that for superintendents and city managers the data would include the "correct" cell of low leadership and high professional attitude. For superintendents, the skewed distribution (they are high on the leadership scale) virtually eliminates any relationship between leadership and professionalism. About two-thirds of both groups (superintendents with low or high professional attitudes) are classified as high on leadership. Since leadership is political, although not as political as Burns would prefer, we have to wonder why the highly professionalized school superintendents are willing to slug it out in "normal" political disputes. It should come as a relief to those who worry about the effects of professionalism upon responsiveness to learn that superintendents are far more willing to wheel and deal than is normally thought to be the case. City managers, thought to be less addicted to professionalism, are also less inclined to leadership. Here, however, they get it "right": highly professional city managers are substantially more likely than less professional ones to be low on leadership. For them, the contradiction between professionalism and leadership exists and is resolved by avoiding leadership. The low leadership-high professional cell is the modal one for city managers. Since superintendents are high on both scales they apparently respond to the contradiction differently.

Superintendents are "professional leaders." They do not necessarily sacrifice professionalism by becoming political leaders. Obviously, superintendents' preferences cause us to wonder about traditional assumptions about their purely apolitical behavior. They are more political than we, and most others, have thought.

Item analysis of the leadership scale discloses that the largest difference in leadership roles between superintendents and city managers is superintendents' attitude that their activity in school elections is good and justifiable. Superintendents are more likely than city managers to agree that they should urge people to run for legislative office or to aid them in their efforts. Earlier research (Zeigler, Jennings, and Peak 1974) had shown that superintendents prefer board members who are "trustees" rather than "delegates." They prefer board members who do not believe they should merely echo the sentiments of their constituents, but should maintain independence. But this does not mean that they were willing to go out and find them. Much of what was suggested by Zeigler was that

active politicking by superintendents would be counterproductive.
Things have changed, however. Today's superintendent seems to
be more willing to take the risk of getting involved in school board
elections.

For Max Weber, professionalization and bureaucratization
were, if not synonymous, certainly coterminous. But because professionals feel the tug between demands of neutral competence and
leadership, they frequently have trouble surviving in a bureaucratic
setting. If the polity suffers because professionals demand autonomy, the professionals themselves suffer if the organization cannot
assist them in reconciling demands. Weber and his followers (see
especially Blau and Scott 1962) rephrase the dilemma. Instead of
assessing the contradictions between neutrality and leadership,
they talk more of problems of loyalty and authority. Professionals
must be both loyal and, simultaneously, be given the authority that
their professional status requires.

Professionals are viewed as beleaguered internally by the conflicting demands of loyalty and deference to authority, and externally by the demands for neutrality and leadership. According to the
logic of this argument, professionals can be truly professional only
when they are entirely disconnected from any constraints other than
those they elect to impose upon themselves. The bitter struggle between physicians and the Federal Trade Commission (FTC) vividly
illustrates these types of conflicts.

Traditionally physicians, along with other professionals, determined their own membership standards and codes of ethics. FTC
rulings against the professional prohibition of advertising challenged not only the economy of the professionals, but, more importantly, their self-image. The dread of physicians gleefully announc-
ing that their clinics were open "Sunday after church" was so real
that the physicians' political action committee, AMPAC, spent a
great deal of money lobbying for "professional exemption" from the
FTC ruling, a decision that is still pending. Professionals do not advertise; merchants advertise. One might also argue that professionals do not lobby, but this argument is hardly persuasive. They
are using the political process to reassert professional values.

The problems of physicians and lawyers are typical of professionals in an increasingly industrialized and specialized economic
market. Historically, as the occupational market became diverse,
each occupation sought to become a profession. In so doing, they

sought to monopolize expertise. Doctors have not had an easy time in monopolizing expertise. Their potential clients are routinely lured away by less prestigious, less expensive healing occupations such as chiropractic. The struggle by physicians against chiropractors has reached serious proportions in several states, with lawsuits alleging conspiracy being filed by chiropractors, and countersuits asserting the responsibility of physicians to inform the public about fakes.

To prevail over persistent competition from "less professional" sources physicians have developed unusually rigid professional standards, a strict educational regimen, and control of credentials by self-regulating professional associations. All of this would come to nothing if medical doctors started behaving like car salesmen, hence the determined opposition to the Federal Trade Commission.

A similar problem has developed for professionals who are not independent, but rather are employed by public or private bureaucracies. Organizations wanted experts, experts needed money, and hitherto "independent" experts became part of massive bureaucracies. Here, too, professional status was used as a defense against challenges to expertise. Professionalism is a way to monopolize a crucial resource. Independent experts, if they wished to remain so, used professionalism to secure a monopoly and guarantee their continued independent existence. Organizational experts, having already given up independence used professionalism in order to secure unchallenged authority. They exchanged loyalty for authority.

Loyalty and Its Problems

Professionals feel less loyalty to their organizations than to their professions. Professional associations prescribe codes of ethics and principles of conduct for their membership, and these codes and principles have a higher claim upon the individual, depending upon the assertiveness of the profession. To those unable to judge, the existence of professional codes of ethics, if accompanied by an apparent commitment to specialized knowledge, carries substantial weight. Prestige is accorded in rough approximation to popular views of the difficulty of the "rites of passage." It is harder to become a physician than a lawyer, and it is (at least superficially)

harder to become a superintendent than a city manager. Presumably, superintendents would have a more difficult time than city
managers in reconciling professional responsiveness with responsiveness to the governing organization. Competing demands for loyalty must be resolved, however.

Gouldner has developed a simple scheme to classify professionals. He argues that "cosmopolitans" can be distinguished from
"locals." Locals are, as the name implies, loyal to their employing
institution. They want to get ahead, and go along to do so. Professional loyalties are subordinate. Locals are said to be "bureaucratically oriented" rather than "professionally oriented" (Scott 1966).
They respond more rapidly and positively to demands of local origin, whether they originate within the bureaucracy or within the
larger governing body.

Cosmopolitans are guided by internalized professional values.
They demand considerable autonomy in order to apply these values.
Although they give passing allegiance to an employing bureaucracy,
they do not commit themselves to a location but to a profession
(Carlson 1962, 1972). One hardly expects to find exact replicas of
each of these two ideal types, but they are useful in understanding
the stresses of professionalism. Given the reform movement's obsession with efficiency, an obsession that has outlived the movement
itself, public organizations should be ready to sacrifice local loyalty
in favor of professional competence. They should willingly concede
their authority for the assurance that the best "treatment" for a particular problem is being selected. If local governments hire cosmopolitans, they should understand that a commitment to professional
values will limit the participation of the elected sector (school
boards, city councils) in the decision process.

This distinction between the cosmopolitan's professional
values and the local government's participation in decision making
illuminates the tension between neutral competence and leadership.
Can a neutral advisor remain neutral when a lay council is about to
embark on a plan that will lead to financial disaster? Can a city manager, for example, not advise "his" council that collective bargaining agreements have driven large cities to the brink of bankruptcy?

It is difficult to imagine a decision in which technology completely whelms politics and nobody loses. Ironically, much of the
professional conflict management advice tries to make exactly this
point; it is possible to have, in the inimitable jargon of the trade,

"'win-win" decisions. Win-win decisions are those in which all participants gain. They are, in short, decisions in which neutral competence is the only legitimate resource. Examples of such decisions invariably are drawn from the private market: you buy a car, you like the car, the dealer makes a profit. But public decisions with no market constraints are not so amenable. For example, students of public choice make the point that rather than having an incentive to minimize costs, public sector managers actually have an incentive to increase their budgets to a greater than efficient size, as their salaries are positively related to the size of the budget. Still, the belief in such schemes is a powerful inducement to the professional faced with conflict. Win-win solutions require that all participants accept the same decision rules: information, not emotion, is to be exchanged. Once this rule is accepted, the *roles of neutral experts and policy leaders are no longer incompatible*.

Wolcott has explained the ideology of technology as consisting of the value of information, the value of rational planning, and the value of progress. The general public can be expected to accept none of these with any degree of consensus. In Wolcott's words:

> The essence of being a good technocrat is to exert control. Regardless of whether that control is directed at predicting and managing particular settings or represents command of a particular area of knowledge, what one needs is information. . . . Technocrats put great faith in information. . . . Arriving at systematic order through rational planning is another central technocratic preoccupation. The Plan becomes all important, an end rather than a means. Everything turns on clearly understood and stated goals and purposes. The same faith that underwrites information-gathering activities underwrites efforts that put that information to good use through rational decision-making. Technocratic endeavor thrives under the banner of the Rational Planning Ideology. . . . To be a technocrat, there is no question that whatever is being done now can be done better. The only question is where to begin (Wolcott 1977, pp. 159–60).

—4—

The Parties to Conflict

The Job of Governing: How Much Conflict?

This chapter begins with a reprise. We ask again the questions: What do managers do? What is the job of superintendent or city manager? There are, obviously, job descriptions instructing them to "provide leadership" and the like. It is more unlikely that such job descriptions would require that they "manage conflict." Yet, many students of government believe that, whatever else they may think they are doing, governors govern by managing conflict: they institutionalize it, mobilize it, channel it into appropriate directions, ignore it, outlast it, or suppress it. The job of government is to handle conflict.

But should one branch of government manage conflict while others address themselves to the technology of problem solving? Those of us reared in democracies rarely give much thought to the tension between democracy (or conflict resolution) and the application of technologies to problems. Hence, the argument that the only job of government is to manage conflict emerges from the tradition of democracy. As we know, this tradition is met head on by the equally compelling theories of scientific management. Recently, however, we have been brought up short. Some American social scientists, such as Mancur Olson and Samuel Huntington, have suggested that democracies are so enmeshed in conflict (principally among groups) that they no longer can govern. They are paralyzed by conflict (Olson 1982; Huntington 1970).

To govern, then, is to do more than manage conflict. Surely industrial democracies have moved beyond mere conflict management. With the exception of the turbulent 1960s, industrial democracies have not suffered serious internal discord for over a century. To govern according to the new "authoritarians," is to make rational choices based not upon existing demands but upon future needs. Even if such needs are not widely seen, and hence not raised in the form of demands, they must be heeded. City planners, armed with massive computer simulations of an ideal future, can barely contain their contempt for those with less vision. Some, who support the idea of governing with an eye toward the future, have selected "soft authoritarian" countries as models. Chalmers Johnson (1981) for example speaks of the political arrangements that promote efficient government:

> The functions of the politicians are to maintain political stability by holding off the demands of pressure groups or political claimants that would contradict or divert the main development effort and by providing space for an elite, highly educated bureaucracy to operate (p. 12).

The link between these "new authoritarians" and the reform movement is apparent though rarely noticed. Both wanted to manage with a minimum of conflict and a maximum of rational planning. The two movements culminated in March and Simon's (1964) pronouncement that conflict was "pathological." In our study, the approach to the "What do you do?" question was disarmingly naive. As can be seen in the first chapter, social scientists can go a long way in making conflict both complex and mystifying. Assuming that most ordinary mortals are not inclined toward obfuscation, we asked our respondents a set of questions requiring that they estimate how much time they spend managing conflict. We did not define conflict for them, and it proved to be unnecessary. Only if superintendents or managers confused us with the faddish "stress management" did we stipulate that they should exclude private conflict.

In any case, superintendents report that they spend about one-fourth of their time managing conflict, city managers, slightly more than one-third. While this difference is hardly staggering, it is consistent with the theory of professionalism previously described. Superintendents are professional; they dislike conflict, and they do not get involved as often as do city managers. If there is a division of labor between the "reigning" board or council and the "ruling" professional, then division of labor works best in school governance.

Whether or not superintendents are "buffered" from conflict by the board, they clearly can devote more of their time to "governing."

From the perspective of educational administration the fact that superintendents work in comparative freedom from conflict is surely agony. The theme of the beleaguered superintendent is, if not dashed, certainly cast in a new light. Superintendents are not as beleaguered as they think. If they think they are bothered by conflict, they should try trading places with city managers. There is, of course, the legitimate complaint that such a simple question (i.e., How much of your time do you spend managing conflict?) will yield a useless answer. Later in the interview we asked for more detailed responses. The respondents were asked to estimate what percentage of their communications with certain others in the governing process was devoted to conflict resolution. The results were consistent with the earlier findings; there is less conflict quantitatively speaking, in the communication of superintendents than in that of city managers. We acknowledge that one really big conflict is worth hundreds of minor ones, which is why we ask about the time spent managing conflict, rather than the number of conflicts. In the meantime, consider the fact that managers estimate that most of their interactions with the city council, representatives of the community, other local governments, supralocal governments, and their own administrative bureaucracies are laden with conflict. With the exception of dealings with other local governments, at least two-thirds of all managers' communications are defined as conflictual. In clear contrast, superintendents' greatest source of stress is their own bureaucracy. Their relations with others are comparatively harmonious.

It is especially noteworthy that intraorganizational conflict is exceptional for superintendents, for this indicates that much of their conflict involves professionals, rather than the lay public and its rep-

Table 4.1 Percentage of Time Spent in Conflict

	Superintendents	City Managers
Local Legislature	35%	65%
Local Community	50	69
Other Local Governments	35	50
State/Federal Governments	50	71
Own Administration	64	72
X̄	49%	65%

resentatives. Look, for instance, at the relationship between superintendents and their boards, as contrasted to that of managers and
their councils. Much of the tension between expertise and responsiveness simply does not appear to be a concern.

Whether one can infer that the tranquil relationship between
superintendents and their boards is a consequence of either party
knuckling under is the next question to be answered. It is possible
that superintendents spend so little time in conflict because they always do what the board wants. Such a possibility is, of course, remote since superintendents have greater access to information and
staff resources than do part-time board members, giving them an
advantage in the policy-making arena. In addition, superintendents
have the advantage of setting the school board agenda. Previous research has shown that when the superintendent's position was
known, the board voted in a concurring manner 99 percent of the
time (Tucker and Zeigler 1980, p. 144). Furthermore, when school
board members were asked, "If the superintendent wanted to
change the educational program and the board disagreed with the
change, how likely is it that the board would eventually approve
the change anyway?", a majority responded either "very likely"
or "fairly likely" (Zeigler, Jennings, and Peak 1974, p. 164).

What can we make of the greater intergovernmental conflict
on the part of managers? Both schools and cities have been subjected to a bewildering barrage of federal and state guidelines, mandates, and the like. Both, for example, are required to comply with
various affirmative action regulations. But both have their own
unique problems. Superintendents rarely encounter the Environmental Protection Agency and city managers do not worry about
mainstreaming handicapped children. Why are superintendents relatively sanguine about their relationship with federal and state governments, a posture that certainly contradicts much of the popular
literature and journalism? To answer this question we examine the
development of the relationship between local bureaucracies and
extralocal governments.

Governmental Intervention

The State Role

We have described the local educational system as consciously
nonresponsive. States, whose presence in U.S. education preceded
that of the federal government by approximately 100 years, have

shown little inclination to challenge local processes. They have, however, been willing to grant legitimacy to those against whom the school is locally buffered. Generally, at least one-third of the revenues consumed by school districts is allocated at the state level, a large sum in comparison with the 8 percent supplied by the federal government. Allocation of state and federal monies is a much more overtly political process than is true in local districts, and locally quiescent groups are more active on the state and national levels. School administrators, so dominant locally, are less influential at the state level than teachers' organizations and other well-established groups that may take an interest in education (McDonnell and Pascal 1978).

The politicization of education, by being thrust into the turmoil and conflict of state decision making, has become an increasingly significant factor as state and local budgets experience greater strain. Even before the drama of the Serrano decision, the financing of schools had become a major concern of state legislatures. Following *Serrano vs. Priest* in 1971 the school finance reform movement escalated. When the flow of dollars began to dry up because of decreased enrollment, the mood for reform became more intense. Struggling over a scarce resource, the coalition between educational administrators and teachers began to splinter and administrators lost influence.

Court suits challenging the equity of state school finance plans that did not substantially equalize the per pupil expenditures across school districts were successful in some states (notably California, Connecticut, Minnesota, and New Jersey), and were unsuccessful in others (including New York, Oregon, and Washington). Even where court suits found state plans to be inequitable, legislatures did not quickly devise new aid formulas to remedy the situation (Levin 1977). It is much more politically feasible to provide more aid to all districts, than to reduce state aid to wealthier districts in order to increase per pupil contributions in districts that are relatively less wealthy (Garms, Guthrie, and Pierce 1978). While state aid to education has increased substantially in some states (especially California) over the past decade, in most states great disparities still exist among school districts in their ability to finance educational programs because the proportion of the state budget targeted for education has not increased to the extent that the state can "level up" across districts within the state.

In addition, in many states it would be difficult to increase financing for education without also escalating the degree of state control. In New Jersey, for example, it was necessary for legislative proponents of school finance reform to pledge support for statewide tests (which would presumably increase accountability) to garner support for a state income tax to finance the new funding formula (Goertz and Hannigan 1978). Perhaps the major reason why states have not been as active as expected is that, unlike local legislative bodies, state legislatures are besieged by a divided school lobby. School board associations disagree with administrator associations; both disagree with teachers over local control, accountability, collective bargaining, tenure, and related issues. Without a united front, the school lobby cannot maintain the level of control to which it has become accustomed.

Additionally, there is an estrangement between local educators, represented by their lobbying organizations, and state experts in school finance, who staff state education agencies and legislative committees. While state-level school finance experts have generally very accurate estimates of the costs and benefits of various reform schemes, they cannot generate much political support for the programs they advocate (Garms, Guthrie, and Pierce 1978). In state politics, expertise is a less valued resource. Further, since most reform schemes imply a redistribution of wealth—taking from the rich and giving to the poor—they encounter the intense opposition of well-established, relatively conservative, and politically durable business interest groups.

While little has been accomplished in the way of reform, a major assault upon the integrity of local districts grew out of this conflict. The "accountability movement" can be attributed at least partially to the growing costs and decreasing benefits of education. It also had its roots in state legislators' disillusionment with the narrow and defensive ideologies of the education lobby, which seemed to focus on increasing educators' salaries without adequate concern for the quality of the educational program. State legislatures, supported by business organizations, were attracted to the notion of holding local districts accountable for their products, while conceding that actual control of districts was well beyond the reach of the citizenry. The most widely used device to obtain accountability is the statewide testing program, vigorously opposed by teachers and administrators, which has nevertheless been enacted by 36 state legislatures (Caldwell 1982).

While educators both at the local and state levels may oppose statewide attempts to increase accountability, the statewide tests may nonetheless serve to focus public attention on the performance of their local schools. A recent 50-state survey showed that a majority of respondents, officials of state departments of education, felt that "local districts should set standards for minimum competency tests" (Caldwell 1982, p. 6). Referring to New Jersey, Goertz and Hannigan report:

> Minimum standards of proficiency were to be *locally* determined; without statewide minimum standards the impact of a statewide evaluation system would be minimized (1978, p. 55).

Still, the point we are concerned with here is not whether the competency movement will ultimately succeed; rather the point is that the participation of the states in educational politics is causing schools to be held accountable for poor public performance. For an educational establishment used to a controlling monopoly on information, this is a serious threat, one that will be resisted at every step of its implementation.

Educators' fear of accountability is directed mostly at state legislatures, as opposed to state departments of education, because they are not under the monolithic influence of educational organizations. Previous state involvement in making educational policy, credentialing teachers, establishing appropriate curricular materials, and the like, has largely come from the state executive bureaucracies, with little if any participation by the legislature. As long as technological hegemony remains in the hands of the educational establishment, superintendents feel somewhat sanguine. The accountability movement, however, has not followed this pattern. Competency-based testing at the state level, then, provides the most politically realistic hope for making school more responsive to the public. In this sense, the goals of the state are politically threatening to the educational establishment.

The Federal Role

On the surface, the federal presence appears even more threatening than the state's to educational administrators. In fact, local educational professionals are far more comfortable with the federal presence than with state intervention. The federal contribution to local finance is not large, and the ability of the federal government to monitor implementation and evaluate results is limited by budgetary problems and inadequate personnel. Irrespective of implementation and evaluation problems, the major thrust of the federal intervention, beginning with *Brown vs. Board of Education* and continuing through to the issue of bilingual education, has concerned equality. Local schools seek to maximize both liberty and efficiency since state systems are anxious to achieve accountability, and the federal system emphasizes equity (Guthrie 1980). It is no wonder local schools are accused of failing to achieve their tasks. Which tasks should they achieve? The goals of efficiency and equity are frequently incompatible. The goals of responsiveness and efficiency certainly are, as are responsiveness and equity.

Toward the latter half of the 1960s as schools came to receive greater attention from national policy makers, they were faced with incompatible demands. The federal government demanded that schools serve as agents of social change, but simultaneously returned the control of schools to "the people." Clearly, although the federal government routinely attaches "maximum feasible participation" codicils to its directives, its essential goal is equity. This type of inconsistency is likely to arise when one level of government gets involved at another level. Where greater local participation results in "majority rule," one result is likely to be the ensuring of the rights of minorities (e.g., the disadvantaged, handicapped, etc.). Local governments seek to conserve, while national governments seek social change.

The intervention of the federal government, then, has had a consistent pattern, whether the source of the intervention has been the courts, Congress, or bureaucracy. The goal is to increase the educational and, by inference, economic opportunities of deprived populations. In becoming the voice of the underprivileged, the federal government has responded to demands that local systems, because of the legacy of reform and the ideology of administration, could not meet. Being deliberately insulated and unresponsive, schools had little established communication with representatives for undereducated populations. As perpetuators of the status quo, they had a vested interest in preferential education. Thus the federal government, the traditional defender of the downtrodden against the conservatism of local community power structures, took the role of advocate for the underdog.

Judicial intervention has been an important influence in the educational system. Busing, the teaching of "black English" to black students, a vast array of student rights and hiring procedures, and even the extent to which school districts must guarantee that a legally prescribed portion of the minority population will be achieving at the level of national norms, are all the products of judicial intervention. The exhaustive detail resulting from the courts' monitoring of busing is stark evidence of the extent to which their control is deeply woven into the fabric of local decision making. Of all the decisions involving the federal role in education, busing is the most visible and controversial. The courts' role is even more significant because political expediency may influence the unwillingness of Congress and the president to allow the Department of Education to withhold funds when school districts fail to comply with busing guidelines. John Gardner, then secretary of HEW, spoke adamantly against local districts' noncompliance with Title VI of the Civil Rights Act of 1964 saying that if found negligent, a district "will be required to take prompt and effective remedial action . . . " (Orfield 1969, p. 172). In 1967, 122 districts not in compliance with Title VI had federal funds curtailed, but this monitoring activity became almost nonexistent within three years, generally due to a lack of support from a new president (Nixon) and Congress (Orfield 1969). Congressional reluctance virtually required that courts rule on busing plans on a case-by-case basis. Thus, in spite of its visibility, and owing in part to the vigorous opposition of white parents, an administrative apparatus to facilitate the process of busing does not exist.

The issue of busing illustrates, especially in the absence of an administrative network, the federal commitment to equity. Congressional reluctance cannot, of course, alter judicial precedent. It can, however, minimize federal bureaucracies' ability to monitor the process. The resort to busing was, in fact, an admission that previous, less drastic devices to insure equity were not successful.

The federal bureaucracy's commitment to education became institutionalized with the passage of the Elementary and Secondary Education Act in 1965. With the exception of judicial intervention, there was no appreciable federal presence until then. The foundation for federal management of educational policy was buttressed by a substantial increase in federal funds, especially in the provision of grants under Title I of ESEA (to meet the needs of educationally deprived children). Title I was supported by minority groups whose local access had been frozen and it was also supported by some segments of the public school lobby (Wilson 1976). Administrators desired an increase in federal aid and were less concerned with the implications of nonlocal control.

As ESEA was implemented, a new pattern of interaction was created, furthering the notion that lay control through school boards was obsolete. Local administrators were unreluctant to hasten the demise of local boards and did not view the federal bureaucracy as a threat to professional hegemony, a correct analysis. To compete for Title I grants, local schools hired administrators to write proposals. When such proposals were funded, more administrators were hired to establish and maintain the programs. Thus a local bureaucracy was expanded to do business with a federal bureaucracy. Relations between the two sets of bureaucrats were cordial and the influx of federal funds was welcome. It is true that audits revealed misuse of Title I grants, but funds were rarely withheld as a consequence of such audits:

> In general, the federal government's oversight effort is not large or rigorous, and USOE seldom identifies instances of non-compliance through the oversight process. . . . Federal oversight thus contributes little to centralized enforcement. A greater federal effort is technically possible, but there is little support for it in either USOE or Congress (Hill 1979a).

This is a minor cost for local officials to bear. In exchange for a modest constraint, they are able to shift their bargaining strategy from negotiations with potentially active local groups to a more sympathetic audience of fellow bureaucrats.

In a recent study of the "Cumulative Effects of Federal Education Policies on Schools and Districts," Knapp et al. (1983) found generally fewer complaints from school administrators about federal programs than anticipated even though a great deal of administrative paperwork was generated as a result of these programs. They noted:

> The people who deal with the administrative detail tend to be those whose salaries are paid out of special program funds, especially program managers in the district office and teaching specialists or aides in the school. In all but the smallest districts, such people handle most of the administrative chores related to federal and state programs, thus minimizing the burden on classroom teachers and principals (p. 7).

The number of complaints also seemed to diminish within one or two years after a given law's implementation. Presumably by this time the necessary staff had been hired and trained.

There is, in fact, a physical interchange between federal and local bureaucracies that further insulates school administrators from local demands. Hill reports on a network of state and local officials whose careers have become focused solely upon the administration of federal programs. School districts maintain large, well-financed offices of federal relations. Although Title I was the initial point of entry, other federal mandates followed. Additionally, compliance with one set of mandates required violation of others. For example, schools sought to ensure that at least half of a "magnet" school's teacher and student population would be black. In order to achieve this, federal rules regarding the concentration of minority staff had to be challenged. Also, federal mandates may conflict with state mandates. In *Authority to Control the School Program*, Van Geel (1976) notes that while the federal government preferred bilingual/bicultural methods of instruction, some state statutes would not allow bicultural programs. In addition, bicultural programs can create semisegregated programs that may be unconstitutional at the federal level.

A comprehensive examination of federal efforts at equal educational opportunity reveals much about the inconsistency of the federal effort, as illustrated by the previous example. As Radin explains

> there has been no agreement on a single strategy for change. Two distinct and often contradictory approaches underlie the federal activity: desegregation (breaking up concentrations of children, whether by court order or through federal funds) and compensation (providing additional resources for children in their existing school setting). . . . The two strategies reflect very different theories about the cause of educational inequality" (1978).

Given the problem of multiple and conflicting demands, local schools are placed in an advantageous position. Virtually all school districts participate in one federal program. A majority receive funds from at least two. Most often, Title I and P.L. 94–142 account for the lion's share of federally funded programs. Additionally, however, there are administrative burdens imposed by the Emergency

School Aid Act, Titles VI and IX of the Civil Rights Act of 1964 (prohibition of discrimination on the basis of race, sex, or age), the Vocational Education Act, and Title VII of the Elementary and Secondary Education Act (bilingual education). There are other regulations, such as the recent Department of Agriculture ruling (based upon its funding of school lunch programs), that "junk food" could be sold only after the regularly scheduled lunch period; however, these sorts of regulations do not require a large implementation and evaluation apparatus capable of sorting out a bewildering and occasionally contradictory set of rules.

There is another advantage to the position of the local district. In spite of the widespread attention given to loss of local control as a consequence of the federal presence, the fact that the programs make competing demands upon local funds requires that districts decide which regulations to pursue most vigorously and which to ignore. In addition, school administrators can use state and federal regulations as a reason for their course of action, whether or not it may be justified, as local lay officials may not understand state and federal regulations enough to know otherwise.

Another interesting facet of this issue is that a superintendent, no matter how vigilant, becomes dependent on staff experts conversant with each of the categorical programs. While the abolition of junk foods and other highly visible federal decisions (e.g., the recent interpretation of Title IX prohibiting dress codes on the grounds of sex discrimination) are symbolic evidence of a federal presence, it is in the dependence of the superintendent upon an expanded staff of federal relations experts that the greatest impact is felt. These staff experts are placed in the position of picking and choosing among priorities. They are, as we noted, frequently trained within the federal-state-local bureaucratic nexus rather than in the tradition of the superintendency. It is to this cadre that the day-to-day administrative tasks will of necessity be delegated. The expert's experts operate with regard to the superintendent in the same manner with which the superintendent interacts with the board—they control information. As Hill explains it, " . . . the multiplicity of federal programs makes it impossible for the superintendent to pay sustained, simultaneous attention to the whole set of federal programs. The result . . . is that the delegation of program management to specialist coordinators is virtually total" (Hill 1979b). For any given district, the federal impact is fragmented and generally ineffective.

Given these Byzantine relationships, it is no wonder that superintendents can stand up to the challenge. They agree, far more than does the local public, that the efforts of the federal government in the direction of equity are worthy (Tucker and Zeigler 1980, p. 64). Superintendents' favorable view of federal and state bureaucracies, a view at odds with rational expectations, is a consequence of "picket fence federalism." Professionals from all layers of government develop consistent and cohesive values. In education, the orthodoxy favors the equity implicit in federal mandates. Hence local superintendents, rather than reflecting the mood of their local constituents, identify with the profession, thus reducing conflict.

In Bailey's view, the legal structure of U.S. federalism makes intergovernmental disputes difficult to define in terms of subordinate or lateral conflict. Superintendents and city managers are creatures of the state. States, in turn, are legally subordinate to the national government. But the pervasiveness of allegiance to the educational profession makes the conflict lateral. As noted by Hill (1979a), in spite of the existence of a federal structure, bureaucratic exchanges at all levels of government minimize the legality and maximize the cordiality of the relationship.

This is not to suggest, of course, that city managers live in constant combat with agents of the federal and state government, but they do see more of an adversarial relationship there. Again, the obvious explanation is lack of professional cohesion. The International City Managers Association is just that. It is unlikely that city managers will establish supragovernmental professional relationships with representatives of various nonlocal bureaucracies. There is certainly an "occupational contact network" provided by various municipal associations, but there are so many functions performed by cities that specialized "subgovernments" (that is, organizations that focus upon a specific policy area) tend to exclude the more generally educated city manager. Planners, fire chiefs, police chiefs, and so on, all have professional associations independent of city managers. Hence, when federal employees of the Environmental Protection Agency appear, there is not likely to be much sharing of common experiences with a city manager.

Local Legislatures

The legislature, school board, or council offers the potential for a major misunderstanding in relations with professionals. Legally, conflict between a legislature and a professional is defined by the superordinate-subordinate relationship. But in reality, there is a strong probability that the conflict is at best lateral (between equally placed political actors) or even superordinate with the "wrong" group (the legislature) on bottom. Much of the reform ideology dealt with the proper role of boards and city councils since they represented, at that time, the most apparent challenge to the ideology of expertise.

It is not entirely clear why the reform movement swept through the field of education without strenuous resistance from those who stood to lose the most. It is true that the machines did not go down without a fight, but they seemed much more concerned with resistance to the reform movement in municipal government rather than in educational government. One possible explanation is that arguments for rational management are much more appealing when discussing the sacred object of the child. In any case, the appeal to trust experts, to depoliticize education, was remarkably successful. The reformers placed great faith in institutions. They believed that institutions could control behavior. Although it is currently fashionable to assume that people and institutions are inextricably intertwined in policy formation and the distribution of influence, the success of the reformers in developing a blueprint for institutional change was remarkable. It is not an exaggeration to assert that the educational reform movement was unique in the extent to which educational institutions controlled the behavior of participants in the educational process.

The number of school districts was reduced substantially—from the more than 130,000 preceding the reform movement to about 16,000 today. Centralization may or may not be more efficient, but it certainly is likely to minimize the ability of a district to respond to a diverse clientele. The inability to respond was heightened by a dramatic reduction in the heterogeneity of school boards. The "best people" soon occupied virtually all remaining school board positions.

In an influential textbook on public school administration published in the early 1900s, Ellwood P. Cubberley, former Dean of Education at Stanford, described the "best people" for board positions. Those deemed suitable board candidates included "men who are successful in the handling of large business undertakings—manufacturers, merchants, bankers, contractors, and professional men of large practice" as these people were accustomed to "depending on experts for advice." The types of people Cubberley did not recommend as potential school board members included "inexperienced young men, men in minor business positions and women" (Callahan 1975, pp. 35–36).

The suddenness of the change is well illustrated in St. Louis where reformers persuaded the Missouri legislature to approve a new charter providing for the reduction of the board from 28 to 12, the elimination of wards, and the creation of a nonpartisan ballot. The charter was approved in 1897. In 1896 professionals and businessmen constituted 14 percent of the board; in 1897 they constituted 83 percent of the board. By 1927, the year of the first systematic survey of the social origins of school board members, the St. Louis pattern had been duplicated on a national scale. The working class had been eliminated and replaced by business and professional elites. It is not surprising that school boards became the exclusive domain of the affluent; after all, reformed municipal governments were similarly staffed. What is worth recalling is that this once was not the case. It is generally assumed that local politics is more likely to be biased to a greater extent toward middle- and upper-class participation (as contrasted to national politics). While this is true, it is more a consequence of institutional structure than any "natural" law. Business and professional dominance of boards after reform also can be explained in cultural terms. Putting aside the beliefs of the reformers that businessmen were superior, possibly by nature, it is true that the period from the turn of the century until certainly the middle 1930s was one in which the culture of business was dominant. Until the depression, the "business of government" was business.

However, the decline of business's hegemony did not seriously retard the continued disenfranchisement of the working classes. In 1968, a year during which the demands for pluralistic political representation were widespread, school boards were as narrowly focused as they had been in the years immediately following the reform movement. Board members, when compared with the general public, possess qualities traditionally more valued and esteemed in American society. Ninety percent were male; 96 percent were white; 45 percent were lifelong residents of the community in which they served; 72 percent were college graduates; one-third had incomes in excess of $30,000; 66 percent were businessmen or were professionally employed; 93 percent owned their own homes; 85 percent were Protestant. In the 1960s, then, the typical school board was virtually a perfect replica of the ideal board as outlined by reformers a half century earlier (Zeigler and Jennings 1974). Such people frequently behave in a way that superficially appears to be opposed to their economic self-interests. In contrast, the less affluent are generally inspired by "ethnic and party loyalties, the appeal of personalities, or the hopes of favors from the precinct captain" (Cubberley 1916). It is precisely for these reasons that reformers sought to change the shape of the local electorate; to substitute public-regarding for private-regarding participation. As part of the local policy spectrum, educational issues are generally less interesting than those generated in state or national elections. Citizen concern centers on economic issues since these are personally salient to the less affluent. During a depression, the public-regarding person can afford not to worry about the state of the economy. His investments may not show their usual profit, but the reduction in standard of living is not great. For those less fortunate, depression means unemployment. State and national governments deal with economic policy. The issues of local politics, such as the quality of education, land use planning, and the like, are of more interest to the well-to-do.

This perception does not deny the fact that local politics occasionally become heated. Educational policy may run afoul of the "margin of tolerance" of a community and generate substantial episodic conflict. Sex education, text censorship, and related issues can cause a community to explode. Nevertheless, the issues of local politics generally are of less immediate concern to all but the public regarding minority. Thus, the upper class dominance of school boards is hardly unique. There are, however, certain aspects of the recruitment process that suggest board members are not typical of the population of elected officials. For the average board member, personal experience with educational administration is common. A majority have some personal link to education—parents or other relatives have been teachers or administrators. The participation of close family members in the educational system predisposes individuals to take an interest in board membership. Board members themselves are likely to have had at least a partial career in education. Thus the occupational involvement of board members in education far exceeds the involvement of the general population (Zeigler and Jennings 1974).

Obviously, family background is a "proximate" cause in propelling some members of the civic elite to seek board membership. More significantly, board members are able to pursue a career in education without much involvement in the overall political process.

Typically, public officials come from "politicized" homes. That is, they are likely to have been raised in homes in which both parents are interested in public affairs, discuss politics, or might be active in political organizations. School board members, unlike most elected officials, do not come from such homes. Additionally, school board members (with the obvious exception of those in large, unreformed cities) regard board membership as a civic obligation rather than as an opportunity for political mobility. If one examines the background of state and local elected officials, it is rare that one will find a school board background. Again, the fact that school board membership is not generally used as a springboard to higher office fits well with the reformers' aspirations.

Clearly the conventional wisdom does not apply to school board members. The reformers' blueprint worked well. The absence of political ambition means that civic duty is the driving force in board members' choosing to run for election. Civic duty, also common among city council members, is the dominant mode of thought in educational politics. In "normal" politics, ambition is the essence of personal behavior and, incidentally, accountability. Ambition is a requisite for meaningful elections and an accountable political process. Without personal ambition, the desire for reelection and upward mobility, elected officials see no need to pay attention to their constituents. Indeed, civic duty dictates that representatives should not be politically responsive, rather they should locate the "true" public interest. Without worrying about constituents, school board members are free to consider "what is best for the kids," a cliché without concrete meaning.

Again, we return to the schizophrenic nature of educational governance. The nominal governors, serving because it is their duty, do not have a clear image of a constituency. Lacking such an image they naturally find it easy to depend on and identify with the bureaucratic, full-time administrative apparatus of the school system. Their representational roles become reversed. This explains why rather than speaking for their publics to the administration, they come to view their role as explaining the administrations' policies to the public. Normal representation thus is not part of the orientation of school boards. The recruitment process predisposes board members to view their responsibilities as resembling more those of the board of directors of a corporation rather than those of a legislative body.

The distinction is not trivial. Legislatures are presumed to engage in conflict resolution, debate, bargaining, and ultimately, decision making. While it is true that legislatures no longer initiate most policy making, the public clearly expects them to respond to conflicting demands and to resolve conflict. To reiterate a major theme, political conflict, regarded as normal and healthy in the legislative process, is regarded as pathological by the educational establishment (Salisbury 1980). Therefore the school board may refrain from dealing with controversial issues (e.g., curriculum, school reorganization, etc.) that the public feels are important.

School Board Representation

The ability of school boards to avoid conflict again provides evidence of the remarkable success of the reform movement. In virtually every phase of their public lives, in addition to their recruitment, boards conform to the reformers' dream of stability and deference to expertise. The pursuit of a generally apolitical life is only a part of the story. Boards, to a higher degree than other local and state elective bodies, engage in conscious self-perpetuation (Zeigler and Jennings 1974). In the absence of political parties or active political groups, prospective board members are frequently recruited by the existing board. Like-minded individuals, those regarded as reliable, are sought as vacancies become available. Of course a fair amount of recruitment by the existing board is necessary simply because serving on the board is a thankless task. Finding any respectable candidates can be a formidable undertaking. Still, incumbent board members recruit to a large extent to ensure stability, to guarantee consistency, and to avoid the election of candidates drastically out of harmony with the prevailing philosophy of the board. Like most public bodies, turnover, especially incumbent defeat, is relatively rare. Combined with a "procession of like-minded men through office," school boards, more than most legislatures, are able to avoid serious policy shifts which could result from unstructured recruitment (Cistone 1975). One commentator referred to the practice of avoiding the risk of random recruitment as "oligarchic self-perpetuation" (Cistone 1975). Clearly it is, but the motives are less to perpetuate an oligarchy than to create a public image of stability.

Boards and superintendents are acutely conscious of their public images. Stability, one essential public image to be created and maintained, is well served by the structures put in place at the turn of the century. Our description of the social origins of board members would be merely interesting were it not for the fact that the agenda of problems to be addressed and the style of board decision making are clearly influenced by the class perspectives of board members. Since a major goal of the reformers was to place board positions beyond the grasp of the lower classes and into the hands of the classes with the greatest sympathy for the professional role of the superintendent, the placing of "good" people on boards was not enough. Such people should understand the principles of good management, an understanding born of experience in business.

This is not to suggest, of course, that all board members are from the same class. However, even in poor districts, boards are made up of the relatively advantaged community members. Surely it is the case that the school board in a rural West Virginia community is less well off than its counterpart in Evanston, Illinois. In both cases, however, the typical board member is better off than the average member of the community. Most importantly, the lower the status of the board (and hence the community), the less likely it is that the superintendent will be successful in getting the board to defer to his/her claim to the legitimacy of expertise. Lower status boards are less inclined to "trust the experts," and they are more inclined to want to involve themselves in the day to day administration of schools. Higher status boards, which after all can lay some claim to expertise at least partially equal to that of the superintendent, may raise more initial objections to administrative policy proposals, but will not offer much in the way of determined resistance. Lower status boards, which may be initially overwhelmed by technical jargon, prove in the long run to be more tenacious in the resistance to expert recommendations. Such boards, which spell trouble for the superintendent, are relatively scarce (Zeigler and Jennings 1974). Once again, the reformers knew what they were doing. The lower the status of the board, the less the possibility of developing consensus about the appropriate division of responsibility between board and superintendent.

Our sample included a large number of suburban communities as well as a few selectively small urban school districts and municipalities. An examination of suburban America is admirably suited to

Table 4.2   Do Legislative Bodies Differ on Role of Manager or Superintendent

"Are there any important differences between what you think the job of a school superintendent/city manager involves and the way the school board/city council sees it?"

	YES	NO	N
Superintendents	40%	60%	52
City Managers	62%	39%*	52
sig = .03			

*Exceeds 100% due to rounding.

test the success of the reformers. While there are ranges in affluence, of course, these communities on the rim of two major cities are generally far better off than each of the central cities they surround. Public professionals should find little of bother here. But such is not universally the case. Taking the question implicit in Bailey's work, we inquired about whether or not there was any dispute about division of labor. Are these managers bothered by boards or councils that interfere in administration? City managers say they are, but superintendents are not. Further, many of the problems reported by superintendents are of an entirely different type. They believe boards expect too much of them, that they are presumed to be omnipotent when (as they confide privately) they are only human and have on occasion made mistakes.

City managers, far more troubled by confusion about roles, lament the unwillingness of councils to leave them alone. There is also a status problem to be gleaned from the protocols of the interviews with managers. They fret that councils do not understand the policy significance of their position and tend to view them as "pencil pushers." In any case, role identification is more bothersome to city managers than to superintendents (see Table 4.2).

In Chapter 3 we noted that actually losing a vote, that is, experiencing a *public* defeat, is relatively rare, far rarer for superintendents than for city managers. But apparent public consensus may conceal the "real" world of behind-the-scenes haggling. Superintendents may not lose many votes, but they lose quite a few arguments. The reason they appear so dominant is that they only go for a vote when they can win; much of their losing is private. William Boyd (1976b) is a proponent of this argument.

Table 4.3   Frequency of Occurrence: Majority of Legislature Disagrees with Manager or Superintendent

"How often do you take a stand that the majority of the board/council seems to disagree with? Would you say this happens often, sometimes, rarely, or never?"

Response categories: rarely and never = rarely/never
                     sometimes and often = sometimes/often

	Rarely/Never	Sometimes/Often	N
Superintendents	79%	21%	52
City Managers	56%	44%	52

Of course no one can really say for sure. In an earlier study, we found very little of the sort of smoke-filled-room atmosphere upon which the "realists" base their case (Tucker and Zeigler 1980). There are only two ways to find out: to watch them or to ask them. When we watched them, we missed it (Tucker and Zeigler 1980). Consequently, in this current study superintendents were again asked about conflicts they face with the board, this time in a comparative fashion. In Table 4.3 we display the response to a question concerning the frequency with which city managers and superintendents face a legislature in which the majority will not support their positions. As was the case with actual voting, hostile majorities do not crop up very often, but city managers face them more frequently than do superintendents.

The process cannot be exactly recreated. Presumably, when managers or superintendents judge that the majority is against them, they can press on, irrespective of the probability of loss, or modify or withdraw their proposal. To do these things, however, is nonprofessional. One may very well have a good sense of a "zone of tolerance," but proposals to the legislative body are not made as "trial ballons."

A more typical strategy is to fall back on professional status. Avoiding hostile legislative majorities is perhaps more easily accomplished when the legislature believes in the competence of the administrator. We are not suggesting another variant of the "trust me or fire me" theme. Rather, we suggest that legislative opposition is most likely to appear when there are doubts about the administrator.

A glance at Table 4.4 provides some evidence for this assertion. Those with strong professional identification face hostile majorities less often than the less professionalized. Of course, one can always argue that strong professional commitments "require" that insignificant opposition exists. In much the same way that surveys consistently overestimate the turnout in elections (since voting is what you are "supposed" to do), perhaps professionals would be less professional than they wished if they admitted to hostile majorities. This does not appear to be a reasonable explanation, however, for the fact is that more professional administrators have more manageable legislatures.

Indeed, a contrary argument fits more closely with the facts. Recall that superintendents spend about one-third of their time in conflict with the school board, while city managers spend about two-thirds of their time in conflict with their councils. Since city managers spend so much time in conflict, professional commitment does not make a great deal of difference: both the professionally committed and the relatively nonprofessional city managers spend a lot of time arguing with their city councils. But such is not the case for superintendents. Contrary to what common sense and social theories of professionalism lead us to expect, the highly professional superintendents spend a great deal *more* time in conflict with their school boards than do the less professional ones.

But breaking the superintendent sample into two groups— those above and below the average reported levels of conflict—we found 43 percent of the highly professional superintendents in the above average group, but only 13 percent of the less professionalized superintendents experience higher than average levels of conflict. In spite of the assumption that professionals do not act like politicians, superintendents do exactly that! They talk like professionals, but they are willing (perhaps out of necessity) to take on the legislature. So professionals can engage in conflict. The most professional superintendents face fewer hostile majorities *and* spend more time in conflict. Perhaps they face less opposition *because* they are willing to confront their boards, but this is only speculation. They also lose more votes, but perhaps they risk more.

None of the data negates the essential conclusion that superintendents have an easier time than do city managers. Not only do they find their school boards more manageable, they also believe

**Table 4.4   Relationship Between Frequency of Conflict with
Legislative Board and Occupation, Controlling for
Professional Attitude**

Frequency of Conflict with Legislative Board	Professional Attitude			
	Low		High	
	Occupation			
	Superintendent	City Manager	Superintendent	City Manager
Rarely or Never	69%	50%	82%	64%
Sometimes or Often	31%	50%	18%	36%
	100%	100%	100%	100%
	(16)	(30)	(33)	(22)

that intraboard consensus is rather high. Two-thirds of the superintendents, as compared with two-fifths of the city managers, regarded their legislatures as having very low levels of intragroup disagreement. The norm of unity is still very much alive in school
boards, though city councils are more rent with disagreement.
School boards are more clubby; members get on quite well with one
another. This cannot be due solely to at-large, nonpartisan elections
(which were, of course, designed to create just this sort of spirit of
cooperation), since the city councils have the same institutional arrangements. Nor can this camaraderie be attributed to the homoge-
neity of the constituency, since school boards represent the same
constituency as city councils. If there is a single plausible explanation, it is probably the pervasiveness of the norm of unity. It is bad
form to make a public fuss if you are on the school board.

Still, there are those who do not go along. City managers, facing a less compliant legislature, also have trouble predicting the
lines of disagreement. The opposition floats, forming and reforming
from issue to issue. City managers are evenly split on the question of
whether they can predict the composition of city council factions,
while 83 percent of the superintendents claim that the opponents
are "always the same people." Since the same people are generally
no more than two (usually one), the traditional stereotype of the
"naysayer" is given some support. Superintendents see stable factions, because the opposition is one or two isolated people who are

just ornery. Superintendents do not regard these individuals as approximating an opposition party. If such a situation were to develop, board-superintendent relations would be seriously jeopardized. We might have expected that city councils would develop into more stable factions, one representing the "loyal opposition." The absence of stable factions means that city managers have a more difficult time managing conflict because they cannot know with any degree of certainty whom to lobby, whom to isolate, and whom to ignore. From the point of view of democratic theory, a loyal opposition is a necessity; but from the view of the administration, it is not. City managers no doubt would relish the opportunity to deal with their opponents as isolated naysayers, as do superintendents.

Committee Structure

Are we really talking about "little legislatures"? Many of those who prescribe for school and city governance suggest that we are poorly served by expecting too much from them. Compared with their counterparts in state and national politics, they are poorly staffed, poorly paid, and poorly trained. Government at the grass roots is supposed to be amateur government, and certainly school boards and city councils are amateurish. One common lament is that the committee system, so well developed in national government, if to a lesser degree in state government, has no tradition in local government. Standing committees are so much a part of the "normal" legislative process that legislative action is unthinkable without them. Such is *not* the case in local politics. Although the trend toward legislative committees is growing in city government, and to a lesser extent in school government, about half of the school boards and city councils do not have any standing committees. Since our sample avoids the largest cities (because they do not have city managers), we understand its limitations. Large city government relies more upon standing committees, but even here there is more use made of the special committee (not necessarily composed solely of legislators). Curiously, since our relatively small districts are divided evenly between those with and those without standing committees, they are just about the same as the boards of large cities, 46 percent of which have standing committees (National School Boards Association 1975, pp. 48–50).

Committees are viewed with distrust among believers in the reform. Standing committees create the opportunity for competing sources of expertise, and presumably the opportunity for factional alliances. In national politics, congressional committees, well-staffed and well-prepped, can make life agonizing for haughty bureaucracies that think they have a monopoly on expertise.

The preferred mode of governance in local politics, especially educational politics, has been to operate without committees, presumably on the assumption that the city manager or superintendent can provide all the staff work necessary to make informed decisions. Implicit in this assumption of course is that committees would increase conflict, a reasonable assumption based on the power of committees in other legislative arenas. Indeed, it seems likely that local legislatures with committees would be more apt to develop hostile majorities than those without them. Presumably, school districts would have fewer committees.

In our survey, neither assumption proved accurate. Both city and school legislatures have about the same percentage of committees: one-half have none, one-fourth have three or fewer, and one-fourth have four or more. Further, there is a significant *negative* correlation between the number of committees and the probability of hostile majorities ($-.22$) and with the number of executive recommendations rejected ($-.31$). There is much conventional wisdom laid to waste here. For once, the reformers were wrong. Committees reduce conflict; they do not exacerbate it.

Why this is the case is sheer speculation. We do believe, however, that there is a fundamental difference between local committees and those in state or national legislatures. Local committees do not have independent staffs. Since staff work is provided to committees by the manager or superintendent's office, the committees may serve to legitimitize decisions. They can serve as the first contact between the board or council and the professionals. Such committees do not resemble those used by state legislatures or Congress. They do not report legislation to the full body; they do not "bottle up" legislation. Finally, executive proposals are not automatically referred to committees by the legislative leadership, since there generally is none. Nor is there evidence that the existence of committees contributes to intralegislative squabbling.

Public Apathy

In education, as in most public enterprises, there is evidence that only a small population gives attention to or participates in the process. Since barely half of the eligible voters bother to vote in presidential elections, it is hardly surprising that fewer than one-fourth take any role, even the relatively passive role of voter, in educational policy making. Normally passive, the lay public and its component interest groups, however, still pose a potential threat to the dominance of experts. Although lack of participation is equated with client satisfaction, such a conclusion (sometimes referred to as the "dissatisfaction theory of democracy" [Lutz and Iannaccone 1978]) is not necessarily warranted. As long as education does not produce demonstrable evidence of failure, it is not likely that lay control will be advanced as a serious alternative.

Administrators, however, face greater risks in education than is true of other public bureaucracies. Just as children as sacred objects inspire deference to expertise, so do they encourage anger when the product is demonstrably inadequate. It is common to hear people lament that schools "are not what they used to be," a complaint generally attributable to nostalgia. In fact, those who complain are right. Schools are not what they used to be. They are far more expensive, and those who consume their services are not as well educated as they once were.

These details are not germane to the argument about the double-edged sword of expertise, but they do justify a modest discussion. The annual cost of precollegiate education exceeds 60 billion dollars, making it the most expensive service performed by either state or local government in the United States. The cost of education has increased at a rate far in excess of inflation, and far in excess of the increase in the cost of other government services. A substantial portion of this increase can be explained by increases in salaries. At the same time, achievement scores have been declining. Scores in mathematics declined about 25 points between 1970 and 1980, while verbal achievement declined about 35 points. Ironically, the percentage of "A" grades more than doubled during the same period (*Public Opinion* 1979).

The institutional changes installed by the reformers occurred before the current uproar over low achievement, but they were ready for it. At-large elections, centralized boards, nonpartisan elections held at strange times of the year (when no other elections are being held) are all devices that ensure minimal public participation.

There is a common thread in these institutional changes: the insulation of schools from political conflict and the substitution of technological skills for political resources. If school boards were to be converted from legislatures to boards of directors, if their role were to become less that of policy initiator and more that of policy ratifier, then clearly school policy initiative should be placed in the hands of professional managers.

It is hard to conceive of a package more explicitly designed to reduce lay control than that resulting from the reform movement. Every conceivable linkage between leaders and followers has been eliminated. The depth of change exceeded that of the more general urban reform movement, of which the school reform effort was an integral part. Historians may argue as to whether school reform grew out of municipal reform or preceded it (the latter point of view seems more persuasive), but there is no gainsaying the fact that the institutional changes of the reform movement were more eagerly grasped by schools than cities. Thus it is the case that only two-thirds of all city elections are nonpartisan, compared to virtually all school elections, and 59 percent of city elections are at large, compared to more than three-fourths of school elections (Tucker and Zeigler 1978).

Cooptation and Interest Groups

One traditional way of controlling conflict with the public is through cooptation. Ad hoc and permanent citizens' committees are relied upon for a great deal of what normally passes as public opinion. Citizens selected to serve on such committees are by no means selected at random from the constituent population. Their backgrounds and values tend to reflect those of the legislators and administrators: they are leaders of the business and professional communities with specialized knowledge and prestige.

Although committees may have been intended to institutionalize conflict, the opposite result has occurred. Unlike legislative committees, which reduce conflict, citizens' committees increase the probability that a superintendent or manager will face a hostile majority. There is a problem with spurious correlations here, but not a serious one. City councils make a substantially greater use of such committees than do school boards. In our sample, there were about eight citizens' committees, on average, for every council and about two per school board. Since city councils are more aggressive than school boards and since they have more citizens' committees, is not the relationship between citizens' committees and a hostile legislature spurious? Or perhaps citizens' committees are created *because* there is more conflict. Although the distributions are precarious, there was enough variability to run this same correlation by occupation. The same result ensued. School boards do not normally use committees, but those that do are more likely to resist the superintendent.

Although this relationship still does not solve the chicken and egg question, at least we can say that citizens' committees are associated with conflict, and irrespective of their intended use, do not reduce tension. Since school districts tend to use these committees in such disputes as school closing, perhaps they might want to consider another method of cooptation. It is curious that these powerless advisory committees, selected because they are "reliable," are associated with conflict. One possible avenue of exploration is to inquire whether they are permanent or ad hoc. Permanence implies a normal, routinized method of communicating with the public (as, for example, on citizens' budget committees), while ad hoc suggests more of an immediate, and possibly cyclical, problem. Most of the city councils' citizens' committee are permanent, but there is no discernible pattern for comparable school board committees. Since they had so few, little can be said except that about half were budget committees and about half were ad hoc. Of the ad hoc, virtually all involved school closures. Irrespective of their nature, such committees also are associated with increased intracommunity conflict. All in all, they seem a bad choice if the goal is to minimize conflict, and a good choice if the goal is to institutionalize conflict. Hence, the greater reliance upon committees by city councils fits well with our description of councils as less reluctant to start a fight.

We should not leave the issue of citizens' advisory committees without placing them within the broader context of interest group politics. Interest groups are said to be a link between rulers and ruled, at least by those who theorize in such matters. The theory has gone through a substantial number of revisions, moving well beyond the primitive notion that "special interest groups" somehow distort the process of representation to more sophisticated arguments about the impact of such groups on public policy and the delivery of public services. Curiously, the argument has come full circle. Originally such groups were regarded as "bad" because they sought to subvert the abstract notion of a "public interest," under the rise to prominence of pluralist political theory. Then they were accorded a rightful place in the process whereby governments are made aware of "demands" and, hence, are able to respond to them. Policy is portrayed as a process whereby governments transform demands into action. Thus, without demands there can be no decision, no policy.

The "good versus bad" argument was entirely rephrased by the work of Mancur Olson. Whether they do or do not represent the views of their members for the purpose of pleading their cases before governments (Olson says they do not), interest groups "reduce the efficiency and aggregate income in the societies in which they operate and make political life more divisive" (Olson 1982, p. 74). Since divisive political life is one of the evils the reformers of American local politics sought to eliminate, Olson's argument is of unusual importance here. He uses industrial democracies as examples of situations in which interest groups reduce efficiency and make political life more divisive. The high growth, capitalist economies of the Pacific (Taiwan, Hong Kong, South Korea, and Singapore) serve as examples of where this inefficiency and divisiveness have *not* occurred. Korea and Taiwan, as colonies of Japan, had no freedom to organize interest groups and, once independent, showed no inclination to encourage their growth. Singapore, long a British colony, had no need for them during colonial status, and has shown no inclination to encourage them since independence. Hong Kong, of course, is still run by the British according to nineteenth-century laissez-faire ideology (while the mother country languishes in the grip of powerful organized groups).

Before concluding that we have taken leave of our senses (what has any of this to do with educational and municipal governance?), recall that these arguments guided the reformers in their determination to de-institutionalize interest groups in local politics. No matter what else they did, interest groups got in the way of the rational planners. Formally organized interest groups, generally regarded as the agents through which conflicting demands are brought to the attention of decision makers, are not a stable part of the local educational system. They exist, certainly, but they are not accorded much legitimacy, nor do they survive for long periods of time. The professionalism of superintendents militates against a normal group process. The higher the education of a superintendent, the greater the commitment to professional norms. The greater the commitment to professional norms, the less likely a superintendent will be to accept the conventions of the normal political process.

Since the reform movement's ideology was less successful in municipalities, we might assume that managers were more likely than superintendents to accord interest groups legitimacy (Thompson 1976). This is indeed the case. The actual mode, as well as the preferred mode, of participation differs. City managers are less likely (38 percent) to regard the dominant form of public participation as unorganized individuals than are superintendents (58 percent). In neither case do organized groups play a major role, but city managers regard the mode of public participation as a combination of groups and individuals (42 percent), while superintendents (25 percent) do not. Cities, indeed, are more attuned to group participation than are school districts. Additionally, or possibly because of this relatively robust group-demand system, city managers (29 percent) are less likely than superintendents (40 percent) to *prefer* individual participation as opposed to group participation. Groups simply have more legitimacy in city politics. Whether or not the more active interest groups common to cities make them less efficient, they probably do make political life more divisive. There is a correlation between the number of organizations and the extent of conflict between the executive and the legislature, a correlation that is strengthened when looking only at city managers, and decreased when looking only at superintendents.

The relatively benign nature of the group process in educational governance is well illustrated by the kinds of groups that most frequently appear there. As you might suspect, the Parent Teacher Association (PTA) is the most frequently listed group, followed by citizens' advisory committees. With all due respect to these organizations, they are virtually auxilliary governments. Citizens' advisory committees are created by the school board, and the PTA, bitterly resenting its image as "cookie pusher," is still a far cry from a real interest group. Leigh Stelzer's comments on the PTA serve as well to describe many citizens' advisory committees for local school districts:

> The PTA, a mainstay of support for many boards, has several obvious drawbacks. The PTA is a creation of school administrations for passing on information—not for articulating demands—and its members are justifiably perceived as boosters. Furthermore, the PTA appeals to a narrow segment of the constituency. Few members, much less outsiders, would seek or expect its support in articulating grievances. . . .
>
> School government could not survive in the face of conflict without developing some kind of coping mechanism. The sensitivity of so many school-related issues is a natural foundation for conflict. The widespread requirement that school governments submit budgets, tax levies, and bond proposals to public referenda assures conflict sooner or later (1975, p. 73).

But there is our own evidence to consider. Thirty-six percent of mentions by superintendents of organized groups were either the PTA or citizens' advisory committees, while 50 percent of the mentions by city managers were business and professional organizations or neighborhood groups. A majority of those mentioned by city managers are *external* to municipal government, while the largest number of groups mentioned by superintendents are *internal*. Nevertheless, citizens' advisory committees do not make life as comfortable for superintendents as their origins and history might lead us to suspect: they are associated with increased conflict. Consequently, when it comes to the task of managing conflict stemming from public interest groups, the job of city manager seems to be more difficult than that of superintendent. However, here it is difficult to ascertain the direction of causality. It may be that in districts that are highly conflictual, school officials are more likely to appoint advisory committees in order to attempt to diffuse conflict.

We wondered whether superintendents and/or city managers might underestimate or overestimate conflict. Speculation on this point abounds. Some have suggested that the heavy reliance of educational researchers on case studies exaggerates the extent of conflict in school governance (Tucker and Zeigler 1980). Additionally, as school governance is relatively free from conflict, superintendents may regard communication as conflictual, while others may not. What may appear as a relatively harmless request for information may be seen by a superintendent as a challenge to authority.

In order to obtain a more rounded picture of superintendents' and city managers' situations, an additional set of respondents were contacted in a subset of the sample. These ancillary respondents represent a cross section of people who have firsthand knowledge about a city or school district. They were board or council members, staff officers, line officers, media representatives, and union leaders. While providing little additional information for the analytical portions of this book, these interviews did give us a sense of the reliability of the responses of our primary respondents. In 90 percent of the cases, the ancillary respondents' assessments of the level of conflict matched those of the primary respondents. This high level of agreement suggests that the chief executives of schools and cities have an accurate understanding about the publics that they serve.

This discussion of the public, the legislature, and interest groups may obscure one important fact of life in public and private organizations: most of the communication is *intraorganizational*. The external communication of public officials attracts media attention, and almost all the writings of political scientists concern extraorganizational conflict. But in the real world of day-to-day bureaucratic life, these events, while not rare, are less memorable to managers than the routines of government. Sociologists have provided most of the work on intraorganizational disputes because of their concerns with authority and bureaucracy.

In the life of a public bureaucracy, who has power within the organization is a more compelling question than how a manager is getting on with the public. Public conflict may be sensational, but intraorganizational conflict affects the heart of the organization. This point is well illustrated by our broad-ranging discussions with managers and superintendents concerning the most important incident that caused conflict for each. In addition to a series of questions about the routines of conflict management, we asked our respondents to recall the single event during their tenure that had created the most problems for them. The respondents were encouraged to be as reflective as they chose, and little attempt was made by interviewers to do more than record the conversations. Our analysis of these conversations allowed us to determine whether or not the incident was "internal" or "external" in its origin. Conflict episodes were internal in origin if they came from line or staff officers or employees, and were external if they came from anywhere else. Of the conflict episodes mentioned by superintendents 85 percent were internal, as were 71 percent of the episodes mentioned by city managers. It is, of course, significant that managers reported more (29 percent) externally originating conflicts than did superintendents (15 percent). But the fact remains that overwhelming majorities of both groups recall internally originating events as their most serious conflict episodes.

Conflicts that start within an organization do not necessarily stay there. Indeed, more than half of the conflict episodes reported ultimately involved the community, and 22 percent of those episodes cited by managers involved the legislature as well (only 9 percent of the superintendents' episodes engaged the board members).

Intraorganizational conflict is subordinate conflict, especially in schools. Schools are an especially appropriate arena to discuss Weber's belief that bureaucratic authority is vested in offices and not in those people who occupy them. "The superintendency," as opposed to a particular superintendent, is the source of power. There seems to be more Weberian thinking in schools than in city governments, where managers are given less deference and hence must rely more upon personal skills.

Bureaucratic authority is based upon expertise, and there are many within a city's bureaucracy who have a greater claim to expertise over service delivery aspects of local government than the city manager. In schools, there is also a discrepancy between expertise in the delivery of the service and expertise in the management of the system. Teachers, like superintendents, think they are professionals. Superintendents thus report *more* conflict with employees. There is, indeed, an employee problem, and it is closely related to the extent and nature of collective bargaining in education. Collective bargaining involves more than work conditions; it involves policy. There is really no comparable group of professionals in city government. Police officers and fire fighters are, of course, in possession of certain technical knowledge, but they did not go to school to get their jobs, as did teachers. Planning agencies come close, and they typically offer the city manager a genuine challenge to authority. This example aside, city managers do not have the same "em-

Table 4.5   Percent of Respondents Noting Moderate to High Levels of Conflict Between Themselves and Superintendents or City Managers

	Superintendents	*City Managers*
Administrative Staff	37%	46%
Line Officers	40%	50%
Employees	48%	40%

ployee problem" as do superintendents given the substantial collective power of teachers. Nor do city managers have as large a central office staff. The average central office staff of superintendents is 15, compared to 10 for city managers. City managers do not necessarily face more compliant employees, but they do enjoy the advantage of supervising the delivery of a multifaceted service. Their employees are diverse and less professional than are the employees of schools. However, while they can expect less professional unity from employees, they may expect more of a challenge from the various department directors. All of this is borne out nicely by our data. City managers report higher conflict with staff and line officers than do superintendents (see Table 4.5). The central office of the superintendent is comparatively tranquil.

Teachers and Collective Bargaining

The policy-making role of teachers clearly has an effect upon their traditional role as agents of implementation. More importantly, while their individual delivery of services was conducted "behind the classroom door," and was only monitored on a sporadic basis, the entry of teachers into the policy process has raised previously dormant questions about accountability. The problem becomes apparent when we consider that the policy impact of collective bargaining transcends the policy process as described in these pages. Prior to the emergence of teachers as a collective political force, they were regarded, and regarded themselves, as "employees" of the district. Legally, this is so. However, there was also an emotional, subjective connotation to the word that links directly to the nonpolitical tradition of education. Like other participants in the system, teachers eschewed politics in favor of professionalism, and generally did not challenge administrative decisions. The National Education Association, the oldest and largest of teacher organizations, had been dominated by administrators prior to the 1960s and stressed the theme of unity. Loyalty and obedience, the values so strongly associated with the superintendent's role, were part of the heritage of teachers.

As late as 1969, Rosenthal asserted that teachers' organizations "play a negligible part in determining school policies. . . ." To be "professionals," in the view of teachers, meant avoiding disruption, especially strikes. They viewed striking as unprofessional and did not regard autonomy as their prerogative. Traditionally, administrators regarded teachers as amenable to their control. Teachers, Corwin reported, found their status acceptable: two-thirds of the teachers he studied claimed that they

> make it a practice of adjusting their teaching to the administration's views of good educational practice and are obedient, respectful, and loyal to the principal. . . . Approximately one half of the sample agreed that their school's administration is better qualified to judge what is best for education . . . one half of the sample agreed that teachers who openly criticize the administration should go elsewhere . . . on the other hand less than half of these believed that the ultimate authority over educational decisions should be exercised by professional teachers (1966).

The conversion of teacher attitudes, from acquiescent to militant, has resulted in a major change in the distribution of influence in school governance. It is certainly the case that teachers' organizations are represented by organizational politicians rather than classroom teachers. Thus, the gap between leaders and followers is substantial. The more active teachers are more militant; such is the nature of interest group politics. However, it is also true that mass attitudes have changed substantially. In the 1960s, a majority of teachers regarded striking as unprofessional. In the 1980s, a substantial majority—perhaps as many as two-thirds—approves both of collective bargaining and striking, when bargaining fails (Elam and Gough 1980).

The process whereby teachers abandoned the notion of the professional as subservient and accepted the idea of the professional as militant is instructive. Even when a minority of teachers hungered for collective action, this minority was urban, relatively

young, and (most important) unlikely to have spent much time, beyond the essential requirements, in schools of education (Zeigler
and Peak 1977). As the population moved more into metropolitan
areas, more teachers with these characteristics were recruited.

It was the collective activity of teachers that posed the first
nonadministrative challenge to the hegemony of local bureaucracies. Although the initial thrust of collective bargaining was focused
upon work conditions narrowly defined, such is no longer the case.
Collective bargaining was well received by teachers, not because of
their salaries, but because they were increasingly frustrated by the
problems of urban education. Especially significant was the intervention of the federal government in the process of integration. The
conversion of inner cities from white to black (not exclusively
linked, of course, to integration), left teachers with a harder job. Additionally, the tenets of the reform movement elevated the status of
the professional manager and reduced the ease of communication
between teachers as implementors and managers as policy initiators. A more subtle federal role in management training also reduced the teachers' beliefs in their ability to control their personal
environments. As we have noted, administrators view federal intervention with pleasure. Whether the federal presence is directed toward policy (e.g., equality) or toward the utilization of research and
development, it is welcome. The exchange between local administrators and federal bureaucrats did not allocate much energy or
money to the problems of teachers, however. Thus the sense of
teacher alienation was heightened (Guthrie 1981).

The thrust of collective bargaining by teachers goes well beyond the typical bargains struck in a labor-management dispute. Although the struggle between labor and management in the 1930s
and 1940s was bitter and violent, labor never asked for control over
products and pricing. This is still the case in private sector bargaining, and most public employees' unions follow this model; they limit
their demands to economic issues (Pierce 1975).

Collective bargaining by teachers has taken a different shape.
They have sought a more active role in policy formation. Part of the
reason for a more expansive scope of bargaining stems from the issues of professionalism and control that dominated the reform
movement. Just as administrators, arguing that school boards
should eschew administration, came to define administration as pol-

icy, so did teachers fail to make a clear distinction between working conditions and policy. As McDonnell and Pascal (1978) explain:

> Teachers' own notions of professionalism further complicate the definition of scope, because they expect to play a larger role in defining their work standards than nonprofessional employees. . . . Organized teachers argue that as professionals they have superior training in the specifics of the learning process than do most policy makers and can therefore more knowledgeably make those decisions that most directly affect the classroom environment.

The intellectual basis of the argument is identical to the one on behalf of superintendents as they sought to reduce the influence of lay boards: those with the greatest command of technology should have the greatest weight in policy formation. Not surprisingly, teachers have been as vigorous in resisting parental influence in professional matters as were administrators of the preceding decades. Since the argument was being made in terms of competing technology, rather than in the more traditional language of expertise versus responsiveness, it was especially threatening to administrators. Pierce compares the two challenges:

> The first real challenge to the hegemony of the educational bureaucracy was the demand for greater citizen participation in educational choices. . . . Because of limited participation by parents and the reluctance of administrators to give [citizens] any real power . . . this movement did little to break administrators' control over schools. It was not until teachers began to organize and use collective bargaining to gain more control over educational policy that the monopoly of the school administrators began to crumble (1975, p. 106).

The crucial point is that the hegemony of administrators was challenged by those who could persuasively argue the superiority of their technology.

Of substantial importance is the fact that the right to bargain collectively was not given by local districts, but by state legislatures, bodies substantially less awed by the professional assertion of management and more sympathetic to the aspirations of teachers. The legislatures of 37 states have legalized collective bargaining, in spite of the opposition of administrators. The lesson is clear, and other previously powerless groups have learned it well: the local district can be outflanked and more sympathetic arenas can be found.

Although the specific structure of collective bargaining statutes varies, the process has some common characteristics. First, bargaining is conducted by professionals. The school board and the superintendent have come to rely heavily upon professional negotiators, as have teachers. Teacher salaries comprise about 80 percent of a district's operating budget; both parties are reluctant to trust such a substantial sum to amateurs. The professional negotiators have consequently emerged as major policy makers and the guidelines established by boards or superintendents have failed to restrain either the bargaining process or the negotiators. Such guidelines for negotiators generally refer only to the limits imposed by the supply of money. Other matters more related to policy are open to negotiation without the scrutiny of representatives normally associated with policy formation. Negotiators representing the board and administration may be willing to trade policy for salary, if given the option. Hence, organized teachers have successfully negotiated a number of policy provisions that have constrained school management and changed the traditional responsibilities of school administrators.

Administrators, especially those who portray themselves as beleaguered, usually feel they have been put in a defensive position by the shift in status of teachers from employees to professional competitors (rather than by any serious competition from lay organizations). Still, the actual policy content of contracts is varied. Virtually all contracts allow grievances to be subject to arbitration. Administrators generally find little to quarrel with over such provisions, as conflict is institutionalized and individual accountability minimized. Other policy-laden provisions (class size, evaluation procedures, responsibility for discipline, and the establishment of instructional policy committees) exist only in a minority of contracts. However, the National Education Association and the American Federation of Teachers both support a national collective bargaining law that would cover not only economic issues, but also the educational mission that is to be carried out. The creation of the Department of Education may add bureaucratic support to these efforts. For the moment, the National Education Association does not rate

Table 4.6 Percentage of Respondents Reporting Moderate to High Levels of Conflict with Staff, Line Officers, and Employees, Controlling for Professional Orientation

	Superintendents		City Managers	
	Low Professional	High Professional	Low Professional	High Professional
Staff	44%	32%	55%	50%
Line	38%	41%	43%	59%
Employees	44%	51%	47%	32%

the probability of success as high, although national and expanded collective bargaining is one of the organization's major priorities.

The volatility of the issue of collective bargaining is well illustrated by looking at the way professional orientation is related to conflict with employees (as compared to line and staff officers). In Table 4.6, we have recorded the percentage of superintendents and city managers reporting moderate to high levels of conflict. Conflict with staff is more of a problem for the less professionalized superintendents than for the more professionalized ones. For city managers the level of professionalism is unimportant, since the overall level of staff conflict is higher. The fact that superintendents with strong professional orientation are able to avoid staff conflict is quite consistent with what has gone before. A professional challenge is best met with a professional attitude.

However, line officers do not respond as well, since they are more removed from the physical presence of the superintendent. In city government the more a manager tries to assert his professional credentials, the greater the probability of conflict with line officers. But in conflict with employees, the distinctions become even more apparent. Professionally strong superintendents engage in more conflict with employees; professionally oriented managers engage in less. We think this relationship is well illustrated by collective bargaining.

Collective bargaining is simply more of a problem for schools than for cities. Fifty-six percent of the superintendents list collective bargaining as the substance of conflict, compared to one-third of the city managers. Professional orientation is not a factor; collective bargaining is objectively more of a problem, not merely a difference in perception. There is, however, the matter of professionalism and perception. The fact that professionalism exacerbates conflict with employees for superintendents and reduces it for city managers gets at the heart of the matter. School superintendents are more threatened by employee conflict and collective bargaining because they strike at the legitimacy of professionalism with its norms of unity.

There is an "educational family" that is shattered by employee disputes. The American Federation of Teachers, which includes only teachers, is still less powerful (nationally) than the National Education Association, which until recently made no distinction between teachers and administrators. In contrast to the united professional family ideology of the NEA, the AFT argued that the interests of teachers and administrators are in direct and unalterable opposition (Tyack 1974). While the old idea of one big happy family in education is dying, its remnants can be seen in the dismay with which school administrators view collective bargaining. In fact, a recent survey of AASA members has found that the majority of school administrators "feel that collective bargaining has had a generally negative effect on the quality of public education, and this group appears to be growing—from 66.9 percent in 1977–78 to 72.6 percent in 1981–82" (AASA 1982). The results of this survey also indicate that the increasingly negative reaction of administrators to collective bargaining may partially stem from its continued growth.

> In what might appear to be a related development, the percentages of respondents reporting increases in collective bargaining agreements for both teachers and principals is growing—separate principal agreements have grown from 13.3 percent in 1976–77 to 17.3 percent in 1981–82; teacher agreements have grown from 62.9 percent in 1976–77 to 70.5 percent in 1981–82 (AASA 1982, p. 32).

It is not the danger of the disruption of work that worries superintendents; it is the challenge to authority, the destruction of the public facade of unity. For city managers, these problems are viewed as less unsettling; collective bargaining is just part of the job.

The extent to which collective bargaining and the implicit threat of shared authority is troublesome to those who jealously guard their power is astonishing. The interview protocols on the subject of collective bargaining are rich, and our coding was extensive and complex. We sought to find out whether the respondent viewed collective bargaining in mechanistic terms, as just another headache, as professionally threatening. It is one thing to regard collective bargaining as a management problem; it is quite another to regard it as a threat to authority, and to the unity that educationists value so highly. One superintendent lamented that "it takes away what most of us have spent a lifetime trying to build, and that's a collegial relationship, and puts it in a conflict matrix." Our conclusion, after independently coding each protocol, was that 44 percent of the superintendents, but only 15 percent of the city managers, viewed the collective bargaining process as professionally threatening. For superintendents, there is more at stake than employee harmony: the issue of authority and unity make collective bargaining the symbol of declining status and declining unity.

There was no relationship between professionalism and a superintendent or manager's view of the collective bargaining process: superintendents simply find it more threatening. But then collective bargaining is also more prevalent in school districts. Forty-six of our districts had collective bargaining agreements compared to 29 of the cities. In these districts with collective bargaining, it is not the threat of a strike that bothers superintendents. Only 18 percent of the districts and cities had actually experienced a strike. Thus, in most cases, superintendents who are threatened by collective bargaining cannot attribute their fear to having lived through an actual strike.

Collective bargaining seems a good way to end the discussion on the parties to conflict. In order to encapsulate the findings so far, superintendents have little to fear from the community, the legislature, or interest groups. For them, the threat is internal. For managers, the reverse is true. They face a more truculent public and a more passive group of employees.

—5—

The Selection of Strategies

When people think about government (which they, of course, rarely do), they are likely to personalize it. Government is an abstraction; a rude cop or a hostile teacher are personal irritations. Managers are professionals, and hence are likely to regard a personal complaint as part of a more general policy problem. If quite a few people complain about police rudeness or brutality, the problem becomes one of policy. Individual complaints can be individually adjudicated, but consistent complaints require a policy change, a personnel change, or both.

We suggest that the clients and the governors operate at different levels of abstraction. This disparity is not necessarily debilitating, but it is time consuming. For example, a 1972 survey (Eisinger) discovered that the complaints of citizens to city councils and mayors were generally quite personal: citizens complained about dog control and other pet problems, traffic control, rezoning problems, and potholes. Citizens seek the redress of individual grievances, and most people approach government when they want something to be done for them immediately.

Eisinger's analysis of the contacts of private citizens with city government illustrates this point quite well (1972, p. 49). He distinguishes between "request" contacts and "opinion" contacts. Request contacts are those that seek the rectification of an injustice to an individual while opinion contacts seek change at a more general level. A plea for help from a black who has been refused customary services by a landlord is a request contact; an allegation of wide-

113

spread discrimination is an opinion contact. Two-thirds of all contacts with city government are of the first kind. People do not think in political terms; generally they demand response to individual problems.

A study of communications in school districts supports this conclusion. The majority of private citizen contacts with school districts requires action at the level of the school, and only rarely is a district policy engaged (Tucker and Zeigler 1980, p. 192). Much of this sort of conflict is easily contained, even if only symbolically. More often than not, managers can indeed "do what the people want" since all they want is individual satisfaction. One good way to avoid general conflict is to resolve problems at the individual level.

It is not our intention to denigrate the resolution of individual grievances. For most of us, this redress is what government is all about. Rather we wish to construct a continuum of conflict, ranging in scope from those conflicts involving a single individual to those involving districtwide or citywide policy. Scope of conflict or scope of policy has clear meaning to managers and superintendents. Rarely do they mention the redress of individual grievances.

Sources of Conflict

For managers then, conflict involves policy. In order to capture as much as we could about the kinds of policies that cause problems for managers, we asked a series of open and closed questions. We began with the "usual" problems that are widely reported in the media. Each respondent was asked to indicate if intervention and constraint, finance, collective bargaining, race relations, and affirmative action were sources of trouble.

Table 5.1 shows that both groups do indeed have similar problems; both are bothered by state and federal intervention, and neither is troubled much by race relations and affirmative action. The relatively low ranking of such visible issues as affirmative action and race relations is not as surprising as it may seem at first glance. Considerable media attention is focused on these issues, because they are presumed to be more controversial than intergovernmental relations, finance, and collective bargaining. But on a daily basis, there is apt to be more stress from working with the more mundane, if persistent, problems.

**Table 5.1   Sources of Problems for Superintendents and
City Managers**

Sources of Problems	Superintendents	City Managers
1. State Intervention	85%	73%
2. Federal Intervention	85%	62%
3. Finance	75%	54%
4. Collective Bargaining	56%	33%
5. Affirmative Action	21%	31%
6. Race Relations	23%	29%
	N = 52	N = 52

But there are also some important differences between managers and superintendents. For once, superintendents appear more beleaguered. A majority of them are bothered by state and federal intervention, finance, and collective bargaining. Managers are less troubled by these problems; in fact, there are significant differences concerning federal intervention, finance, and collective bargaining.

Even in those areas in which groups agree that things could be better, managers are less troubled than superintendents. Why might this be the case? One explanation is that managers have been dealing with other governments and unions longer than have superintendents. Cities are legally creatures of the state, as of course are school districts. But the legal similarity is lost in the realities of financial and political control. About 40 percent of municipal revenues come from state and federal aid; the majority of this aid is federal. This federal largesse is not new. The federal government began to give direct grants in aid to cities in the 1930s, and such grants have been expanded in each succeeding decade. Although Dillon's rule specifies that cities are subordinate to states, cities look more toward the federal government for money.

Just the opposite is true of education. Although there has always been some modest federal contribution, only in the past two decades has the federal government made any substantial commitment to education. Even now only about 10 percent of the money needed to run schools comes from the federal government. Unlike cities, however, most school districts get close to half of their revenues from the state. Because education is a state, rather than a federal responsibility (because it is not mentioned in the federal Constitution), states have played a greater role in the shaping of educational policy than has the federal government.

Thus meddling by extralocal governments is both a newer and more aggressive trend in school districts than in cities. The well-established financial contribution of the federal government to cities has helped to moderate the severity of financial crisis. We are not suggesting the benevolence of federal money, merely its long-established presence. Indeed many would argue that federal money has contributed to the decline of the cities as politically independent units, in much the same way that state money has reduced the independence of school districts. Both cities and school districts are annoyed, sometimes outraged, at other units of governments, but the outrage seems greater in school districts.

There is more outrage about collective bargaining among school superintendents than among city managers for much the same reasons: collective bargaining is a way of life for both, but it is a newer way of life for school districts. School managers are particularly distraught over collective bargaining when they see it erode their control over district affairs. They also view it as an intrusion on the model of the school establishment as a professional family. In both these examples, the attack upon insulation has damaged the governmental unit with the greatest tradition of independence—the school district. However, it should also be noted that the existence of a problem related to collective bargaining was the only problem source that superintendents and managers were asked about (i.e. including finances, state regulations, etc.) which was found to be significantly related to "would consider leaving present position" for both superintendents and city managers.

When left to their own devices, neither managers nor superintendents volunteer that intergovernmental relations are bothersome. Rather, their open-ended responses indicate rather clearly that, in spite of the decline of independence in school districts and cities, most of the conflicts are strictly local.

Managers and superintendents were given the opportunity to reflect upon conflict in three open-ended questions. They were asked about the substance of any disputes with the community, the legislature, and in an especially opportunistic question they were asked: "Consider the specific incidents that have caused conflict to occur during your tenure. Now take the most important incident and discuss how you handled it."

In response to these three questions, superintendents not once mentioned intergovernmental relations. Superintendents responded that the public is more angered by poor service delivery, that the school board is bothered by service delivery and labor disputes, and that the major conflict was over either budget reductions or labor disputes. There was some heterogeneity in the responses of superintendents. For city managers, there was one policy area that dominated all others: planning and zoning. Planning and zoning emerged as the major source of tension with the public, the legislature, and, not surprisingly, as the substance of their most serious conflicts.

There is irony here. School districts are supposed to deliver a single service—education. Yet much of the conflict concerns ancillary responsibilities other than the service of providing education. Cities are supposed to deliver a multitude of services, yet almost all of the conflict revolves around a single area: planning and zoning. Judging from the sorts of policies that cause problems, cities appear to be just as much a single service organization as are schools.

Planning and zoning departments pose the greatest professional threat to the role of the manager. City planning departments are laden with experts, and the tension between these experts and lay persons is often extreme. Planning is the functional equivalent of the curriculum in educational politics. It employs a mysterious language, and is supported by an ideology. Early city planners, usually engineers or landscape architects, were concerned largely with the physical development of the city and the use of land. In recent years, planning has taken on a more exotic aura. Planners stress the "ecology" of urban life and talk of anticipating needs, preparing for unarticulated demands, in short, developing a comprehensive plan for the life of the city. Not that planners are Orwellian big brothers, but they tend to think more in terms of an ideal future than most employees of city governments.

In school governance, planning the curriculum is of a similar nature, with one major difference: the curriculum is far less an object of controversy in school governance than is planning in city governance. Even with the national focus on effective schooling in the early 1980s, there is little meddling in the school curriculum. This domain is left to the educational experts. Parents do care and on an individual basis may articulate their preferences for their children. But school board meetings are unlikely to be used by parents to gain support for one curricular choice over another.

Depth of Change

Of additional interest is an analysis of the severity of conflict, irrespective of its content. Planning and zoning may cause more severe conflict than dog leash laws. There is also more to be learned from examining the severity of conflict rather than solely its substance. School systems and city governments must make decisions of diverse magnitudes and impacts. Organizational theorists have addressed the problem of types of decisions, with varying degrees of clarity. Their goal is to classify decisions along a continuum ranging from almost purely routine to those that alter fundamental goals. Downs uses the notion of "depth of change." There are minor changes in everyday behavior which can be made without changing organizational goals. However, new organizational purposes require (theoretically) changes in day-to-day behavior (Downs 1967, pp. 167–68). Agger, Goldrich, and Swanson offer a useful elaboration:

> An *administrative* demand or decision-making process is regarded by its maker or participants as involving relatively routine implementation of a prior, more generally applicable decision; it implicates relatively minor values of a relatively few people at any one time and has "technical" criteria available to guide the technically trained expert in selecting one or another outcome as *the* decision. A *political* demand or decision-making process is thought to involve either an unusual review of an existing decision or an entirely new decision, it implicates relatively major values of a relatively large number of people and has value judgments or preferences as the major factors in determining selection by "policy-makers" as one or another outcomes as *the* decision (1964, p. 45).

Readers will no doubt note the similarity between these thoughts and the reformers' desire to separate policy and administration. But it is no longer clear whether superintendents and city managers prefer to limit themselves to "administrative" decisions. Earlier work on the concept of depth of change has been inconclusive. Tucker and Zeigler examined all public requests in eleven school districts for nine months. A majority of the requests received by school boards dealt with policy issues. They requested actions that required changes in districtwide policies, rather than adjustments in the behavior of a few individuals.

**Table 5.2   Relationship Between Level of Ideological
Component of Conflict and Occupation**

Ideological Component	Occupation	
	Superintendent	City Manager
Low	37%	46%
Medium	10%	21%
High	53%	33%
	100%	100%
	(51)	(52)

By classifying requests according to scope, we proposed a policy orientation continuum. At the individual level there are few direct policy implications. A person seeking the redress of an individual grievance is simply asking that his or her case be considered and resolved. A parent may request that a child be transferred to another school. This request can be handled without involving more than a single individual. However, a request for a reconsideration of the district policy on student transfers has clear policy implications (Tucker and Zeigler 1980, p. 190). Most statements at school board meetings (and city councils) are, if there is any policy component at all, likely to be represented at the high end of the policy continuum. However, most private communications with superintendents are likely to be at the low end. Superintendents hear far more individual complaints and far fewer policy-related demands than do school boards.

Given these findings, and given the argument that superintendents are more professional than city managers, it is reasonable to suspect that much of their conflict is of the administrative type, as defined by Agger, Goldrich, and Swanson; the "depth of change" was presumed to be low.

The principal investigators individually reviewed each response to the major conflict question, coding for the number of people involved, the scope of the demands, and the stakes involved. High levels of intercoder reliability prevailed, persuading us that we were on the right track. Stronger evidence of the reliability of our procedure is provided, however, by the results shown in Table 5.2. We substituted the terminology of "ideological component" for the more frequently used "depth of change," but the idea is identical.

As can be seen, superintendents face a more ideologically flavored form of conflict than do city managers.

On the surface, this finding is puzzling. Superintendents face less conflict than do city managers, spend less of their time worrying about it, and yet, when major conflict occurs, it is far more than the routinized, rational, goal-setting type that we have been led to expect. Managers, who encounter more conflict, are less likely to confront a conflict in which ideologies are engaged. More conflict does not necessarily mean more intense conflict.

Several explanations are possible. One of the most plausible is that *because* conflict is "normal" in city government and not in school government, it tends to be less ideological. Since conflict is discouraged in educational governance, there are fewer institutional mechanisms to channel it, and more of a belief that conflict is dangerous. If conflict occurs rarely, it is likely to take a relatively major episode to "make conflict happen." Whatever the explanation, it is important to understand that, when measured in terms of intensity or depth of change, school districts do not appear to be as tranquil as when conflict is measured simply in terms of frequency of occurrence. Conflict may not occur as often, but when it does the perceived stakes are greater in schools than in city governance. If conflict were "normal" perhaps the engagement of ideology would be less frequent.

But there is more to ponder. Much of the literature addresses the need to "contain" conflict and stresses the fact that education is a "family" enterprise in which disputes should not be given a public forum. If school governance follows this dictum, why is conflict so much more ideological? Public-oriented conflict should be more ideologically freighted because the public does not know the "rules." But such does not appear to be the case.

In addition to coding conflict episodes according to their source, we coded the substance according to whether it referred to an intraorganizational or extraorganizational matter. As one would expect, the majority (53 percent) of the conflicts reported by superintendents are intraorganizational while a larger majority (62 percent) of those reported by city managers are extraorganizational. This classification does not mean that portions of the community do not ultimately become involved; it simply means that the substance of the dispute had to do with matters largely internal to the organization. Intraorganizational disputes, however, are not the same. In school districts, such disputes tend to be far more ideological than is the case in city governments. As we have seen, collective bargaining has much more of an ideological component for superintendents than for city managers; and much of their intraorganizational disputes involve collective bargaining. At the same time, most of the external disputes of city managers involve planning and zoning, an issue which (while it contains the potential for ideological conflict), often involves the routinization and rationalization of existing decrees. Thus, the "family" disputes of education are relatively serious while the public disputes of city managers are not.

Strategies, Attitudes, and Behaviors

Presumably a repertoire of conflict management strategies would depend on, among other things, the nature of the conflict. But it would also depend upon the predilections of the individual. Some people relish conflict while others loath it; some are Machiavellian and others less manipulative. Henry Kissinger is perceived as cynical and manipulative; while Jimmy Carter appears weak or wishy-washy. Getting beyond these stereotypes is difficult and our approach was as bumbling as most. We began with the assumption that there are certain management styles that are consequences of personal attitudes, preferences, or personalities. Some people appear to be aggressive and combative while others do not. Courses in "assertiveness training" or standard texts on personality attest to the rather obvious fact that some people are pugnacious and others are not. Some enjoy power; others shrink from its use. We do not intend to survey the literature on personality, for we are concerned less with why attitudes toward conflict develop than with how they influence its resolution.

Our groping led us first to routine paper-and-pencil tests about conflict, the most prominent being the Thomas-Kilmann instrument. Administrators are said to develop a "dominant style" (Blake and Mouton 1961) or an "orientation" toward conflict that allegedly shapes their behavior when conflict occurs. Proponents of this view argue that these various styles do not necessarily predict how a manager will behave—there are always questions of strategy and tactics—but rather how he or she will "code" information and respond to demands. Richard Nixon was incapable of responding

"rationally" to conflict because, among other problems, he saw opposition as a threat to his authority (some say masculinity). Nixon
would probably have made an excellent Bolshevik; Lenin certainly
would have made a terrible president.

The Thomas-Kilmann instrument places conflict management
orientations into five categories—competing, collaborating, compromising, avoiding, and accommodating. The authors of the instrument provide the following description of these five orientations:

> *Competing* is assertive and uncooperative—an individual pur-
> sues his own concerns at the other person's expense. This is a
> power-oriented mode, in which one uses whatever power seems
> appropriate to win one's own position—one's ability to argue,
> one's rank, or economic sanctions. Competing might mean "stand-
> ing up for your rights," defending a position which you believe is
> correct, or simply trying to win.
>
> *Accommodating* is unassertive and cooperative—the oppo-
> site of competing. When accommodating an individual neglects
> his own concerns to satisfy the concerns of the other person;
> there is an element of self-sacrifice in this mode. Accommodat-
> ing might take the form of selfless generosity or charity, obey-
> ing another person's order when one would prefer not to, or
> yielding to another's point of view.
>
> *Avoiding* is unassertive and uncooperative—the individual
> does not immediately pursue his own concerns or those of the
> other person. He does not address the conflict. Avoiding might
> take the form of diplomatically sidestepping an issue, postpon-
> ing an issue until a better time, or simply withdrawing from a
> threatening situation.
>
> *Collaborating* is both assertive and cooperative—the oppo-
> site of avoiding. Collaborating involves an attempt to work with
> the other person to find some solution which fully satisfies the
> concerns of both persons. It means digging into an issue to iden-
> tify the underlying concerns of the two individuals and to find
> an alternative which meets both sets of concerns. Collaborating
> between two persons might take the form of exploring a dis-
> agreement to learn from each other's insights, deciding to re-
> solve some condition which would otherwise have them com-
> peting for resources, or confronting and trying to find a creative
> solution to an interpersonal problem.
>
> *Compromising* is intermediate in both assertiveness and
> cooperativeness. The objective is to find some expedient, mutu-
> ally acceptable solution which partially satisfies both parties. It

falls on a middle ground between competing and accommodating. Compromising gives up more than competing but less than accommodating. Likewise, it addresses an issue more directly than avoiding, but doesn't explore it in as much depth as collaborating. Compromising might mean splitting the difference, exchanging concessions, or seeking a quick middle-ground position (1974, p. 12).

The instrument includes forced choice statements which are *not* mutually exclusive, on the assumption that there is a little bit of each orientation in each of us. Thomas and Kilmann argue that these orientations can be understood as dimensions of two characteristics: degree of assertive behavior and degree of cooperative behavior. Here is how these characteristics appear:

Behavior	*Uncooperative*	*Cooperative*
unassertive	avoiding	accommodating
	comprising	
assertive	competing	collaborating

Compromising is a category that does not fit easily into any cell in this table. Thomas and Kilmann view compromising as a backup measure when expediency is necessary or when mutually acceptable solutions are possible. It is not regarded as a particularly distinctive style in its own right. This is a curious interpretation of compromise, which most political scientists view as the heart of the political process. However, since the Thomas-Kilmann categories were developed to study managers, not politicians, this interpretation is understandable. Far more interesting is the use of these categories as guides to professionalism in attitude and behavior. Professionals cannot be unassertive; thus they should not be avoiders or accommodators. They should be assertive, but to be "really" professional, they should be collaborators. The collaborating style is more in the textbook tradition of professionalism than is the competing style, although the temptation to "pull rank" is probably severe among professionals.

Keeping in mind that any one person can combine all of these characteristics, our manipulation of the data leads us to conclude that the dominant orientation for superintendents is collaborating/competing; the dominant mode for city managers is accommodating/competing. Thus superintendents array themselves on the more professional of the two continua, while city managers are more schizophrenic, choosing less professional strategies. Superintendents who are collaborators are "the most" professional, those who prefer a competitive mode are less so. At the risk of losing some of the sharpness of the data, it is fair to say that the "typical" superintendent is, while relying upon both competing and collaborating styles, somewhat more inclined toward the latter. The typical city manager is an accommodator, a mode of management eschewed by superintendents. In terms of statistical significance, the groups differ on these two characteristics: superintendents are more likely than city managers to prefer collaboration; city managers are more likely than superintendents to prefer accommodation. Neither group is likely to select the avoiding strategy, a fact which runs against the grain of those who assume that superintendents regard conflict as dangerous. They may do so, but they have more sense (at least in their abstract attitudes) than to try to wish it away.

The collaborative bias of superintendents and the accommodating preference of city managers illuminates the distinction between the two groups at different stages of professionalism.* Our data also show that the most professional managers, irrespective of occupation are significantly more likely to favor a collaborative orientation. Highly professional managers are anxious to impose their judgments; failure to achieve one's goals signals a lack of confidence in administrative judgment.

Do collaborators collaborate, and accommodators accommodate? It is one thing to profess, it is another to perform. Without worrying about specific conflictual events, we asked our respondents to describe how they resolve conflict. The responses were coded as closely as possible to the management styles described by Thomas and Kilmann.

We took each respondent through the stages of conflict, asking that they describe what they did. Each of their acts was recorded, then compared with the descriptors provided by Thomas and Kilmann. Obviously, there is an element of subjectivity in the work, but the task was surprisingly straightforward.

---

*While both the traits of "accommodating" and "collaborating" are on the high side of the cooperativeness dimension, "collaborating" is much higher on the assertiveness continuum. Hence superintendents generally rate higher on assertiveness.

Before plunging into these strategies, a word of warning is appropriate: these descriptions of strategies are empirically unrelated to the profiles in the Thomas-Kilmann scheme. An individual's description of a repertoire of conflict management strategies bore no resemblance to his or her profile. Collaborators were more likely to actually collaborate than accommodators. Perhaps most importantly, there were no behavioral descriptions of conflict management techniques that remotely resembled the prescribed characteristics of accommodators. Further, the differences between superintendents and city managers were not those one would have predicted from examining the Thomas-Kilmann profiles.

It is commonly assumed that conflict can be minimized by keeping it confined to an individual and avoiding a spillover into policy which might attract the attention of organized groups. Superintendents are in a better position to do this than city managers, because their services involve the well being of individuals more than do those of city managers.

As seen in Table 5.3, although the majority of both groups tries to confine conflict, superintendents do indeed have more of an opportunity to do so, leaving city managers with the more unsavory tactic of cooptation or burying those causing the conflict in a maze of bureaucratic regulation. Of course many conflicts simply resist individualization. When this occurs, the conflict needs to be regulated, controlled, or channeled into appropriate arenas. Much of this can be accomplished by anticipating that a passive grievance may become an active conflict. By this means, a manager enhances his or her ability to regulate the expansion of conflict. In the jargon of the texts, successful anticipation is called "proactive" conflict management (as distinguished from a reactive stance). Anticipation allows managers to maintain control of the agenda, some control over the participants, and, hence, some control over the outcome. If managers simply react, much of this advantage is lost.

Both managers and superintendents use the collaborative style to anticipate potential conflict far more than any other. There is some avoidance, but generally the strategy is to keep an ear to the ground. The technique is hardly mysterious. To anticipate you keep your eyes and ears open, schedule public discussions, visit with employees and clients, hit the rubber chicken circuit (as attending dinners for public relations purposes is commonly referred to by officials), conduct surveys, and so forth. There is little of a Machiavellian nature here.

Table 5.3   Conflict Management Strategies

Methods Used to Individualize Conflict		
	Superintendents	City Managers
Collaborate (Work directly with individual)	66%	55%
Compete (Coopt/Kafka*)	28%	37%
Compromise	7%	10%

Methods Used to Anticipate Conflict		
	Superintendents	City Managers
Avoid (Use staff to shield you from conflict)	19%	24%
Collaborate (Lengthy meetings, discussions, data collection, trial balloons)	70%	69%
Compete (Lobbying, cooptation)	11%	7%

Methods Used to Regulate Conflict		
	Superintendents	City Managers
Avoid (Use staff, postpone action)	14%	19%
Collaborate	48%	48%
Compete (Assert authority and expertise)	8%	7%
Compromise	31%	26%

*Sending an individual through a bureaucratic maze in order to discourage him/her.

When superintendents describe how they regulate conflict, it appears to be a straightforward affair with public meetings, study commissions, and citizens committees. The most significant finding is that despite their strong professional commitment, superintendents are more likely to compromise than are city managers! This unexpected result is made more problematic by the fact that we are still talking about abstract conflict management strategies. The respondents are explaining what they do in general; hence the opportunities for giving a "textbook" answer are apparent. In our research, superintendents often responded that they establish differences and establish areas of agreement. Thus the strategies on which the craft of the consultant rests do dominate. Beneath all of this subterfuge lies the fact that, whatever they may have been told about professionalism, superintendents appear willing to compromise. Perhaps the response is made less meaningful when we recall that superintendents do not experience much need to compromise, as their boards are less aggressive than are city councils. Yet their conflict, less frequent, is more ideological. Compromise comes hard to ideological disputes.

It is possible that superintendents are less stuffy professionals than they appear. Perhaps there is more complexity in behavior than is revealed either in the Thomas-Kilmann inventory or in the description of conflict management repertoires. In looking over the Thomas-Kilmann information, the abstract conflict management repertoire, and the responses to major conflict episodes, we thought that there was an underlying, more fundamental, distinction to be made. The absence of any genuine accommodation in the abstract conflict management inventory strengthened this belief. We therefore decided to cut the data according to the conceptual distinction proposed by March and Simon (1957). They characterized behaviors as either "technocratic-analytic" or "political-bargaining." Technocratic-analytic behavior is characterized by reliance on expertise, staff information, professional norms, and bureaucratic lines of authority. In other words, it is rational behavior. Political-bargaining behavior involves lobbying, negotiating, compromise, giving a little to get a little. It distinguishes between what is professionally desirable and what is politically feasible.

Lineberry and Sharkansky (1971) point out—and we agree—that the two modes of conflict resolution are not mutually exclusive. If the technical-analytical method is rational, then the political one is not irrational but rather nonrational. It takes into account biases and prejudices not reflected in the purely technical strategy. Because managers are presumed to be professionally qualified, they may be presumed to hold political-bargaining techniques in low repute; indeed, the political style is more natural to elected officials—the wheelers and dealers who must take into account the anxieties,

Table 5.4   Relationship Between Conflict Management Style and Occupation

Conflict Management Behavior	Occupation	
	Superintendent	City Manager
Political	39%	27%
Technocratic	61%	73%
	100%	100%
	(51)	(52)

fears, and aspirations of their constituents and not become slaves to the rational planning of bureaucracies. Recently, however, public administration texts have begun to suggest that there is more to managing than being technically competent (Lineberry and Sharkansky 1971). Conflicts that are ideological require more than cost-benefit analysis. School closure decisions uninformed by the preferences and values of clients will be resisted, as will planning and zoning decisions, no matter how logical they appear.

Sheer survival may depend on bargaining and compromise in spite of the preferences of the manager. Our data strongly support this idea. In describing their major conflict episodes, superintendents, more professional than city managers, are also more likely to adopt political strategies (see Table 5.4).

The absence of any relationship between professional attitude and conflict management behavior provides additional support for the idea that superintendents and managers adjust to the demands of the conflict situation. The relatively weak association between occupation and conflict management behavior (albeit the opposite of what one would have predicted), and the absence of any relationship between conflict management behavior and professional attitude strongly imply that conflict management strategies are situational; that they vary with the nature of the conflict and are not controlled by personal preferences. Recall that the major conflict episodes of superintendents tend to be intraorganizational and more ideological than the external and less ideological ones of city managers. Perhaps the response to these conflicts, rather than the characteristics of individual managers or superintendents, is the key to understanding conflict management behavior. Such appears to be the case. Political strategies are more likely to be used in extraorganizational than in intraorganizational conflict.

Table 5.5   Relationship Between Conflict Management Style and Content of Conflict

	Content	
Conflict Management Behavior	Intra-organizational	Extra-organizational
Political	17%	46%
Technocratic	83%	54%
	100%	100%
	(47)	(56)

Examination of conflict management behavior and the ideological component of the conflict yields a similar conclusion (see Table 5.6). The more ideological the conflict, the more political the conflict management behavior.

Some of the findings seem counterintuitive. Intraorganizational conflict is treated technologically even though (for superintendents) it is highly ideological. Yet highly ideological conflict is treated politically. If we break the categories again, combining ideological import and whether the conflict is internal or external, a more plausible set of interrelationships seems apparent. Intraorganizational conflict, usually with a low ideological component, rarely attracts a political response from either city managers or superintendents. Intraorganizational conflict with a high ideological component stimulates a political response more often from superintendents than managers. Extraorganizational conflict with a high ideological component stimulates a political response, more often from superintendents than managers. Extraorganizational, with a low ideological component, motivates more of a political response

Table 5.6   Relationship Between Conflict Management Style and Level of Ideological Component of Conflict

Conflict Management Behavior	Ideological Component		
	Low	Medium	High
Political	23%	31%	43%
Technocratic	77%	69%	57%
	100%	100%	100%
	(43)	(16)	(44)

from superintendents than managers, while highly ideological, external conflict creates a highly political response from managers but not superintendents.

Thus knowing both the content of the conflict and the ideological substance of conflict helps more in understanding conflict management behavior than solely looking at professional attitude. Perhaps this is all to the good. If superintendents really did what they say they do, meaning that they merely administer and are not politically oriented, they would probably finally achieve the high rate of turnover that they fear so much. In fact, they seem to utilize politically oriented strategies in resolving conflicts, rather than merely relying on technocratic solutions. If city managers were really as docile as they claim to be, cities would be rudderless. However, they also seem to apply political methods to municipal conflicts.

Earlier in the book we described the recruitment patterns of superintendents and city managers, calling attention to the rigid professionalism of superintendents. If we see how these recruitment patterns relate to conflict management style, the point is reinforced. Upwardly mobile managers and superintendents are *more* likely to adopt a political style of conflict resolution than are those who have a less clear pattern of career development. They also report less conflict with the public and with their legislative bodies. They are professionally ambitious yet are politically astute.

The upshot of this discussion is that there is more to be learned from behavior than attitudes. The adage holds here: Action speaks louder than words. Still, the words deserve analysis. Superintendents and city managers must present themselves as experts to the publics that they serve and must further express their views on managing conflict in order to instill confidence in and provide legitimacy for their leadership. But if, in the face of intense conflict, the chief executives do not accommodate, collaborate, bargain, compromise, and otherwise respond to divergent positions, they incur the risk of accelerating conflict beyond the issues at hand. As we described earlier, conflict is embedded in our social fabric. Whether these conflicts are contained or expanded depends largely on the craftsmanship of the chief executives in schools and cities.

—6—

Future Trends in Educational Conflict

Our findings confirm that there is generally little responsiveness or conflict in school governance, both in an absolute sense and relative to that found in municipal government. While our study indicates that even in a period of declining enrollments little change is taking place in school governance, others feel that drastic changes are imminent. Guthrie has succinctly described plausible future trends as follows:

> The electoral base for public schools will continue to shrink. Competition for resources will become more pronounced. Decisions about public education will become more politicized and centrally made. Conflict within the education community itself may intensify (1981, p. 75).

We agree that there are important new trends in the demographic, financial, and political arenas that must be considered. However, we do not expect these factors to bring about a "new politics of education" as other scholars have predicted.

Demographic Trends

Fluctuating enrollments may present a challenge to school administrators. By the end of this century, U.S. public school enrollments are expected to have increased substantially. Meanwhile, many districts still face the prospect of closing schools due to declin-

131

ing enrollments. The General Accounting Office has estimated that over 1,200 schools will be closed between 1979 and 1984, with twice that number having already been vacant during the 1978–79 school year. In New York State one out of every ten schools has already been closed, or will be closed shortly.

When asked to describe a major conflict that occurred in their present positions, superintendents frequently discussed conflicts involving school closures. In "The Politics of Declining Enrollments and School Closings" (1982a), William Boyd presents an excellent summary describing why conflict intensifies during times of decline:

> First, resource allocation decisions become far more difficult in decline. The contest, as Behn noted, is no longer "over who should get how much of the expansion of the [budgetary] pie, but over who should be forced to absorb what share of the cuts. . . ."
>
> Second, participation is intensified. Consistent with research on decisionmaking showing that humans weigh losses more heavily than gains, retrenchment activates wide and intense participation as all organizational members and beneficiaries feel a personal stake in the decisions to be made.
>
> Third, retrenchment decisions are complicated by considerations of equity and entitlement. The problem here goes well beyond the well-known fact that staff layoffs according to seniority tend to conflict with affirmative action objectives. . . .
>
> Fourth, morale plummets in declining organizations. Incentives for performance and promotion and career opportunities all tend to dry up. Talented people, who by definition are mobile, tend to abandon the organization for greener pastures (1982a, p. 233).

For all of the above reasons, school closure decisions seem to occupy an important place among the conflicts that superintendents must manage.

School Closures

The question of whether the politics of school closures differ greatly from school politics as usual, with regard to the relative power of the superintendent and school board, still remains unset-

tled. A number of political scientists have commented that nonroutine or episodic conflict is likely to result in the greater relative influence of lay boards in decision making, especially where the issue is
fairly visible, as with school closures (Boyd 1976b; Peterson 1974).
Zald has suggested that "It is during the handling of major phase
problems, or strategic decisions points, that board power is most
likely to be asserted. It is at such times, too, that basic conflicts and
diversions both with the board and between the managers and the
board are likely to be pronounced" (Boyd 1975, p. 107).

Contrary to this expectation, even when superintendents in our
sample described major incidents involving school closures, they
rarely reported that the major conflict was between themselves and
the local legislative body. Conflicts between the superintendent and
the school board were less frequent, both routinely and during major conflict episodes, than for their counterparts in municipalities.
Even where school children, teachers, and administrators are to be
moved and a neighborhood school is closed, conflict between the
school board and the superintendent is still much less frequent than
that between city councils and city managers over major conflict incidents involving planning and zoning. This jibes with the general
results that superintendents face less conflict with the board than do
city managers with city councils.

One possible explanation for the lack of conflict with the school
board even during school closures stems from the superintendent's
expertise in orchestrating participation, as noted earlier. (In fact,
during the interviews a number of superintendents drew an analogy
between their jobs and those of orchestra leaders.) Educators with
classroom experience have learned how to get a class to work as a
whole when many students would rather deviate from the lesson.
This experience is probably helpful for those who become principals
when they attempt to get the faculty to cooperate or when they need
to confront angry parents. By the time superintendents have
reached their positions they have probably had many years of experience in influencing people to follow their game plans, perhaps at
the same time acting as if they had themselves been led. It is no
secret that superintendents often determine policy while making
sure that board members get credit for those same policy decisions.

A superintendent in a much earlier study (Masotti 1968) explained why superintendents, with control over both information
and the board's agenda, are generally able to secure the board's sup-

port for their policy recommendations while still preserving the image that the board sets policy: "It is agreed that the superintendent will submit policy proposals to the board for its approval and then he will administer it; they seldom disapprove of a policy proposal because they haven't sufficient information to evaluate the consequences of the alternatives" (Boyd 1975, p. 117).

When asked how they handled school closures, many superintendents responded that they formed citizen advisory councils to study the issue, set up other public forums to allow people to voice their concerns, and then after a certain number of years (usually two) they closed the schools they had originally planned to close. From some of the superintendents interviewed it seemed that the real issue was not whether or not a school (or set of schools) would be closed, but rather how long they would have to wait until those opposed to the decision within the community had become "talked out." Superintendents also often stated that after the first school closure or set of closures, subsequent closures within the district drew much less controversy.

While one might expect that school closure decisions would create more controversy between superintendents and their lay boards, there are possible explanations to suggest why the data lead to a different conclusion. First, while school closures involve decisions to be made about school facilities and therefore might be expected to elicit angry outcries from neighborhood parents and other citizens, they also have an impact on the school program. Thus, school administrators can claim more expertise in these pedagogical matters than the local citizenry. This is especially true when a change in grade reorganization occurs concurrently with the school closure. Secondly, the list of plausible criteria for making school closure decisions is lengthy, with no clear method for weighting these criteria. Therefore, it is difficult to prove that a superintendent's school closure plan is not based on some sort of rational criteria. As one example, the school board in one Illinois district, Champaign, listed the criteria they used for assistance in school closure decisions as follows:

(1) Convenience: minimize the amount of discomfort caused sending students to a new school;
    (a) minimize students' average walking distance;
    (b) minimize the number of students who would have to be bused (the district followed a policy of busing all

students who lived more than 1.5 miles from their
nearest school);

(c) reduce traffic hazards by keeping the number of
busy streets students would have to cross to a minimum.

(2) Geography: minimize the impact of the school closings upon
the community;

    (a) try to keep schools open where most students walk
to school rather than being bused;

    (b) maintain integration programs;

    (c) examine the potential of the area around the school
for expansion of school-age populations;

    (d) examine zoning laws to see if an area might change.

(3) Facilities: close the buildings in most need of repair and
least able to be adapted for future needs;

    (a) examine the enrollments and capacities for schools
that would remain open;

    (b) examine the size, age, and physical condition of the
building (Yeager 1979, p. 299).

Due to the fact that a school closure has a broad impact and
that decisions to close a number of schools simultaneously necessi-
tate examination of the joint effects of such closures, Robert Yeager
developed a computer simulation to facilitate exploration of the impact of school closures in relation to the above-stated criteria. He
states that the simulation was helpful in forcing the school board to
clarify their assumptions and in illustrating to the public the complexity of the issues surrounding school closures. However, in the
end Yeager concludes:

> The school board's final decision did not appear to be affected
> by the data generated by the computer simulation. For exam-
> ple, one of the schools selected for closing had the greatest addi-
> tional walking distance of any school in the district. More de-
> tailed data bases and more sophisticated projection techniques
> may be necessary for professional administrators who must im-
> plement detailed plans. But the Union Four experience indi-
> cates that, at the decision-making level, hard data create more
> issues than they resolve (Yeager 1979, p. 311).

A similar conclusion was reached by Colton and Frelich in an
exploration of school closure decisions in St. Louis.

> Do school officials in large cities adhere to the growing body of professional lore about "good practice" in closing schools? That is, do they base their school closing decisions upon efficiency criteria such as student-classroom ratios and unit cost of operation? Do they initiate comprehensive citizen participation and public information programs in order to secure at least minimal support for closings? Our observations of St. Louis, which has closed 22% of its elementary schools in the past decade, suggest that they do not. Neither the efficiency model nor the community involvement model has been evident in the school-closing process in St. Louis (1979, p. 396).

While such conclusions may be true, they are nonetheless very difficult to prove. For example, while Yeager's own neighborhood school was closed despite parents' objections and one of the schools closed resulted in the greatest additional walking distance compared to all other schools in the district, it is likely that the schools closed received an unsatisfactory rating on at least one of the criteria listed by the board and it would be difficult to show conclusively that that particular criterion was undeserving of a high priority. Therefore, if a superintendent can win the board's acceptance of a school closure proposal, eventual implementation of the school closure plan is almost assured.

Of course, there are notable exceptions. One such exception took place in Seattle, Washington. The school district administration approached the problem of school closure as a "straightforward exercise in rational planning and decision making. [However,] try as they might to manage the consolidation of facilities as a purely technical problem, political considerations inevitably intruded" (Weatherley et al. 1981). The city's approach was more political. At one point a member of the city council advocated broad community participation in decision making to replace the purely technical style of the school board. The school board president deplored this effort to make school closures a political issue (Weatherley et al. 1981). Commenting on this episode, one of the study's authors drew attention to the difference in ideology revealed by school district and city government officials in approaching the same problems. He alleged that the recruitment and socialization of superintendents requires that they adopt an "insular, technical role" in contrast to the city's broader, more political view (Elmore 1981).

Other notable exceptions include New York, Cleveland, and Chicago. After receiving substantial pressure from community and employee interest groups, school officials in these large urban districts backed down from several plans to initiate school closures in response to sharply declining enrollments. School closures in Chicago, as one might anticipate, were especially controversial:

> Chicago schools' enrollment in the 1970's dropped from a high of 573,000 students in 1971 to 477,000 in 1979. Although hundreds of temporary classroom units were removed from school yards, hardly any buildings were closed. Everytime the general Superintendent proposed closing a building, a delegation of parents, often led by an alderman or helped by school employees, would storm the Board of Education and cause such a furor that the proposed closing would be shelved. The cost per pupil rises in half-empty schools with a full complement of custodians who in Chicago are assigned to schools by a formula based on the square footage of the building (Cronin 1980, p. 4).

Geographical Influence

Due to the fact that employee and community groups seem to be able to thwart school closure decisions in urban districts, we agree with both Boyd (1982a,b) and Iannaccone (1979) that the political tone of school closures in urban, suburban, and rural districts varies. After that point, however, a debate between Boyd and Iannaccone emerges:

> Iannaccone (1979) has argued that variations in political patterns in declining districts can be explained best in terms of the traditional politics found in various kinds of school districts. While Iannaccone's interpretation is persuasive regarding urban school districts, it is less convincing when applied to suburban districts and still less so when viewed in relation to the overall social and fiscal context of public education (Boyd 1982b, p. 241).

Our data tend to support Iannaccone on this point, though Boyd has raised some important issues. In other words, we do not feel that the politics of declining enrollments result in a new politics of education as Boyd argues, but rather politics as usual.

With regard to urban districts Iannaccone claims:

> The political nerve hit by declining enrollment problems every-where—one of its universal political aspects—is the somewhat hidden political tension already present in the local political sys-tem. The unique aspect of the largest cities is their capacity to hold the lid on until the explosive nature of the situation de-mands the involvement of other governments, national or state, and several branches of these governments (1979, p. 426).

This statement, along with the studies of Cronin (1980) show-ing the reluctance of urban school officials to initiate school closures unless forced by financial exigency, helps to explain why urban school closures (or the lack thereof) have resulted in such messy fi-nancial and political conditions for those districts. Urban school dis-tricts tend to receive a relatively high proportion of their funds from federal and state sources. Lately, however, many urban school ad-ministrations claim that locally borne educational costs have in-creased rapidly, partially due to underfunded federal and state man-dates. This underfunding has been especially apparent to urban schools dealing with students with special needs since they have a disproportionately large share of this student population. It is also extremely difficult for urban school officials to raise property taxes due to municipal overburden and the fact that many of those who tend to support public schools, the relatively wealthy, the well-edu-cated, and parents of school-age children (Hall and Piele 1976), have since moved to the suburbs.

Cronin has suggested that the major causes for bankruptcy in Chicago and New York City were the difficulties involved in raising property taxes and the temptation "to try to 'finesse' a deficit by engaging in short term borrowing with tax exempt municipal bonds for just as long as the rating services will allow" (Cronin 1980, p. 15). In addition, the seeming inability of urban school administrators to bring about school closures in Chicago, New York City, and Cleve-land created financial turmoil in these districts. While the behaviors that led to such financial crises for these three urban districts stem from urban school politics as usual (see Iannaccone 1979, pp. 423–26), the results seem extreme. Chicago and New York City school officials lost much of their autonomy to state-dominated financial control authorities. The state of Ohio denied Cleveland the right to even threaten to close schools for a month or more (Cronin 1980), though such closures had been devised to avoid major fiscal difficulties.

What is not clear is whether or not these urban school officials behaved irresponsibly. Some might argue that school officials should have started with plans to close one or two schools rather than proposing multiple school closures and inciting the opposition of community and education interest groups. However, at least one urban school superintendent has stated that this method of "divide and conquer" might prolong conflict rather than minimize it, especially when the opposing interest groups are institutionalized, such as employee unions (as in Chicago) and established citizen groups (as in Seattle). In addition, with regard to deficit financing, urban administrators might argue that they have often borrowed against an uncertain future when state and federal aid payments were late or the amount was yet undetermined. They might also argue that legal constraints limit their flexibility in making budget cuts when future revenue is expected to be insufficient.

Whatever the reasons or motives of school administrators in these urban areas for not adapting better to declining enrollments, their actions resulted in bankruptcy and receivership. Cronin aptly describes the predicament:

> Great cities or their schools do not face bankruptcy without profound repercussions. Financial institutions lend money only to organizations that avoid risks. Parents lose confidence in schools that do not open on time or whose teachers won't work in times of turbulence. Newspapers give city school budget crises front page coverage, causing genuine problems for Governors and legislators, who most of the time avoid treating education issues as "political" (1980, p. 12).

Therefore, contrary to Boyd's statement, if a new politics of education has resulted from declining enrollments it appears to have occurred in these urban districts, not in suburban districts as he asserts.

Furthermore, while the reasons Boyd gives for a new politics of education in declining suburban districts seem theoretically plausible, data from this research project do not support them. Especially with regard to middle-class suburban school districts, he states that "there is strong evidence that declining enrollments has produced a distinctively new politics of education." Boyd states:

> Iannaccone contended that declining enrollments have not created a new politics of education but rather have simply produced pressures exposing existing cleavages and activating the traditional patterns of politics found in different kinds of school districts. Quite to the contrary, however, there is strong evidence that declining enrollments have produced a distinctively new politics of education. First, decline has dramatically increased the frequency of redistributive politics. In the past, middle-class suburban school districts usually were able to confine their politics to distributive issues, whereas urban districts, due to their greater social heterogeneity, were prone to generate conflict-producing redistributive issues. These differences in patterns of political issues affected how middle class management resources were used in urban and suburban settings. Now, however, suburban districts, as well as urban districts, are confronting frequent redistributive decisions. The plentiful management skills of middle-class suburban populations, which used to be employed mainly to minimize conflict, now are being used, in substantial part, to mobilize conflict—that is, to resist cutbacks (1982, p. 241).

If there really were a new politics in suburban schools we would expect to see some evidence of conflict between the board, at least partially representative of community forces opposing school closures, and the superintendent. Most of the fifty-odd superintendents interviewed as part of this conflict management research project were from middle-class suburban districts. Yet when they described conflicts regarding school closures superintendents rarely indicated that members of the school board were on the opposite side. It is conceivable that this phenomenon may be partially attributable to the fact that since superintendents regard conflict between themselves and the school board as abnormal they neglected to report it, but it is unlikely that this is a major explanatory variable. Rather, school closures in suburban districts are carried out according to school politics as usual. The school board serves to legitimize the superintendent's policy proposals rather than acting as a representative of the community (Zeigler, Jennings, and Peak 1974).

Accommodation to Budget Cuts

The foregoing discussion indicates that while school administrators may spend more time managing conflict during times of declining enrollments and budget cutbacks, they still seem to dominate lay boards. A recent *American School Board Journal* article reported results of surveys with school board members who were asked where they would make cuts if they had a 30 percent reduction in the budget. The most popular response was the "executive administration" (Underwood, Fortune, and Dodge 1982, p. 21). However, empirical studies show that when actual budget cuts were made in districts with declining resources and enrollments, administrators were not the first to be axed; classroom teachers were (Freeman and Hannan 1975, 1981; Anderson and Mark 1977). In a more recent study, Anderson and Mark (1983) have concluded that, in fact, "It appears to take relatively large reductions in budget growth to force districts to alter the processes by which the administrative component grows regardless of enrollment changes or budget growth" (p. 8).

Still, declining enrollments and shrinking budgets do result in increased tension within the district, especially when decisions regarding reductions in the teaching force must be made. Seven of the superintendents interviewed regarded this as a source of conflict between themselves and teachers in the district. The same number noted conflicts with teachers over whether decisions about reductions in force and other personnel assignments should be made on the basis of seniority or merit. While distinguishing among teachers on the basis of merit has received favorable attention from the present administration, and has even been put into practice in a few (mostly wealthier) school districts, it seems unlikely that it will gain widespread acceptance as the major criterion for making decisions regarding reductions in force. One reason for this is that judging teachers on the basis of merit creates conflicts for the principal or for other personnel making those decisions. Principals, most of whom do not have tenure as administrators, generally do not welcome this additional source of conflict. Principals tend not to favor "merit" either because they do not feel they have the time or qualifications to make such judgments or because of the "psychic costs" involved. They pressure superintendents informally to advocate "seniority" as the basis for policies on personnel assignment and reduction in force. Researchers who have studied this issue have concluded that seniority rather than merit is more efficient as the primary criterion in making reduction-in-force decisions. Otherwise it may be difficult for teachers to concentrate on the task of teaching rather than on the uncertainty of their jobs (Johnson 1980; Murnane 1981).

While most collective bargaining contracts include seniority as the primary criterion for reduction-in-force decisions, some contracts include provisions to also consider merit and areas of specialization (Johnson 1982). In addition, districts need to consider equity in reduction-in-force decisions since minorities tend to be among the last hired as teachers and minorities and women tend to be among the last hired as administrators. Trying to appease these competing interests when laying off personnel is likely to be unsuccessful. Conflict at the bargaining table may be especially likely to erupt over whether newly hired teachers in special state and federally mandated programs or more senior "regular" classroom teachers should be retained (Encarnation 1982).

Staff layoffs also make the job of administrative leadership more difficult in a less direct way. More than one-fifth of teachers surveyed by the National Education Association in 1981 stated that job security was a principal reason for deciding to become a teacher. The number of teacher layoffs occurring recently might reduce the pool of applicants for teaching positions. In New York City in the mid-1970s the majority of teachers who were laid off due to budget cuts did not want to resume their positions when given the opportunity. Gordon Ambach, Commissioner of Education for New York State, noted that the number of applications for provisional teaching certificates has dropped approximately 70 percent in seven years (Ambach 1983). Across the nation, bachelor's degrees in education are anticipated to drop by 40 percent between 1972–73 and 1986–87 (Kirst and Garms 1980, p. 63). The NEA survey also indicated that less than a majority (46 percent) of teachers surveyed probably would teach again if given the choice again, compared to 74 percent only ten years earlier. Those enrolling in teacher certification programs presently score among the lowest on SATs of students in all college and university programs (Kirst and Garms 1980), adding to evidence that school districts are losing their ability to attract quality teachers. The difficulty that districts are having in attracting math and science teachers due to competition from higher paying jobs in the private sector is especially disturbing in a society which is becoming increasingly technological.

In some districts, private schools have caused deeper cuts into already dwindling enrollments. In addition, competition for students has increased among public school districts. One suburban upper-middle class district in northern New Jersey actually began to advertise for tuition-paying students so that the present staff and programs could be retained. (Needless to say, this effort was not welcomed by school officials in neighboring districts who were also coping with declining enrollments.) Similarly, principals in Chicago have competed for students within the district as an attempt to stabilize their enrollments and the breadth of their school programs (Morris et al. 1981). A few special education teachers in the New York City public schools have remarked that special education programs which previously received little support from building administrators have been given higher status within those schools, since the special education enrollments have kept the district from closing the school.

Some administrators have used declining enrollments as an opportunity to build programs, for example in special or adult education. In Great Neck, New York, the enrollments for the adult education programs totalled 12,000, while only 7,000 students were enrolled in the K–12 program (Eisenberger 1978, p. 36). Periods of decreasing enrollments can, therefore, also be a time of constructive change.

Increasing Enrollments

Changing demographic trends heighten the importance of the conflict management function in school governance. Demographers have recently estimated that the school-age population may increase by over 15 percent between 1985 and 2000. More than a 5 percent increase has been forecast for the period from 1985 to 1990 (Sherman 1982). Since this forecast is predicated largely on the number of children who have already been born, a high degree of accuracy can be assumed. Of course, substantial differences exist among the geographic regions in the United States. As one might expect from population shifts generally, a large increase in school

Table 6.1   Change in School-Age Population by Region, 1985–2000 (Percent)

Region	1985–1990	1990–2000	1985–2000
New England	− 1.7	+ 10.2	+ 8.3
Mid Atlantic	− 6.0	− 6.2	− 11.8
Great Lakes	+ 0.4	− 1.0	− 0.6
Plains	+ 9.1	+ 10.8	+ 20.8
Southeast	+ 7.2	+ 16.7	+ 25.1
Southwest	+ 14.1	+ 27.9	+ 45.8
Rocky Mountain	+ 20.6	+ 33.2	+ 60.7
Far West	+ 11.1	+ 21.2	+ 34.6
United States	+ 5.3	+ 11.7	+ 17.6

Source: School Finance Project, U.S. Department of Education.

enrollments is anticipated in the South and the West with relatively stable or declining enrollments in the Northeast and Great Lakes region. (See Table 6.1 for a summary of the enrollment projections by region for 1985–2000.)

It is conceivable that due to another baby boom, enrollments may start to increase sharply in those very districts that recently closed schools due to declining enrollments. Boyd (1979) has pointed out that school officials in lower socioeconomic-status districts fortuitously saved themselves from conflictual situations related to declining enrollments because the district could not afford to construct new schools; they leased or purchased mobile classrooms which were later easily liquidated. Similarly, administrators who had the good luck or foresight to lease school buildings rather than to sell them may have also spared themselves some conflict as well as saving the district the cost of building new schools. Henry Levin, a scholar in the field of economics of education, has argued that little is saved by school closures and that smaller schools may in fact be more efficient (1983, p. 24). Parents of school children, generally the strongest supporters of school bond levies, may not be hearty advocates for public schools if their neighborhood schools have recently been closed in spite of their opposition. Also, bonds levied for school construction are generally difficult to pass due to the recession, high interest rates, and decreasing support for public schools. More important is the fear that resources to be allocated for education will not keep pace with the anticipated growth in enrollments from 1985–2000.

Financial Trends

Many educators are pessimistic about the ability of the education sector to maintain its share of the governmental pie. Kirst and Garms point out that between 1965 and 1975 "the average proportion of all public expenditures spent on welfare has doubled, and health expenditures have increased by nearly a third, whereas education expenditures have decreased by over 20 percent" (1980, p. 66). A recently completed congressionally mandated study of school finance has concluded that state and local expenditures for education have continued to decline since 1975, while state and local expenditures earmarked for health, hospitals, and welfare have increased by approximately the same amount (Sherman 1982). Samuel Halperin suggests that the problem of decreasing resources for public schools is a political one:

> As education's traditional student body diminishes in number, and as the politically powerful demands of the aging mount— along with other high social priorities—will education's share of GNP be politically able to keep pace? Not without a thorough restructuring of education's tattered alliances and a radicalization of the teaching profession (1979, p. 10).

If the problem is a political one, will increasing rather than diminishing enrollments be part of the solution, or a source of greater problems?

While total budgets may have decreased in many districts due to declining enrollments, nationwide expenditures per pupil (in adjusted dollars using the consumer price index) actually increased by 20 percent over the past decade. However, that does not mean that school districts were 20 percent better off or even that they were necessarily in a better financial position at the end of the decade than they had been at the outset. One reason for this is the high proportion of fixed costs in most schools. For example, if an elementary school with two classrooms per grade loses 20 percent of its enrollment it is unlikely that they will be able to save on building costs, maintenance costs, teacher salaries or the salary of the principal just because the enrollment has been reduced. (Personnel costs represent 75 to 80 percent of the total school budget.) Consequently, expenditures per pupil climb rather sharply. At the same time, state aid, which is based on enrollment, will decrease. This puts more of a financial burden on local taxpayers. Politically, it is often difficult to maintain local financial support for schools where few citizens have school-age children.

The type of school or district described above, suffering from declining enrollments but unable to reduce its fixed costs (e.g., by selling a school, decreasing the number of teaching or administrative positions, and so on) is likely to be better off with increasing enrollments. This is, of course, contingent on state aid per pupil remaining constant. This, in turn, means that in states where enrollments are increasing, a greater proportion of the state budget will be devoted to education, *if* state aid per pupil is to be maintained. This, as Halperin advised us, depends on the political muscle of advocates for education.

Districts that previously reduced their fixed costs and now face increasing enrollments may have to build new schools or perhaps, renovate those that have been leased and altered for other purposes. Consequently, the cost of adding a certain number of additional students is likely to be higher than the average per pupil cost for this type of district. Therefore, these districts may face tighter financial constraints as enrollments increase despite the additional state contribution each extra pupil generates. So what might have seemed a solution to the problem of fiscal crises due to declining enrollments in previous years now only aggravates the financial situation for these school districts. Thus, increasing enrollments per se will not necessarily ease financial pressures now faced by declining enrollment districts. To make this determination one needs to look at the present resource configurations of specific school districts.

Fiscal problems appear to be rampant in today's public schools. As stated earlier, a full three-fourths of superintendents reported financial problems compared to only half of city managers. In a national 1981–82 survey of the members of the American Association for School Administrators (AASA), almost 60 percent reported that their district had reduced the number of teaching positions due to budget cuts. One-fifth of those who reported such cutbacks stated that reductions in federal aid played a major role in the decision (AASA 1982).

When one looks at the recent projections of funding prospects made by the School Finance Project of the U.S. Department of Education, the future looks less than rosy (see Table 6.2). In those states that are expected to have an influx of new students, funding pros-

Table 6.2   Composite Index of Student Educational Need

State and Region	% Children in Poverty 1980	% Children Served as Handicapped Fall 1979	% Limited-English-Proficient Children Fall 1980	Index of Educational Need	Classification on Educational Need Index
United States	15.2	9.2	5.8		
New England					
Connecticut	11.0	10.5	5.1	8.5	Moderate
Maine	14.5	10.0	3.1	11.0	Moderate
Massachusetts	12.7	12.4	3.8	11.0	Moderate
New Hampshire	8.3	5.3	3.1	6.0	Low
Rhode Island	12.7	9.8	4.5	10.5	Moderate
Vermont	11.8	10.3	2.2	8.0	Low
Mideast					
Delaware	13.9	11.4	2.4	11.0	Moderate
District of Columbia	25.4	2.5	2.5	12.0	High
Maryland	11.6	11.6	2.2	8.0	Low
New Jersey	13.4	11.0	6.3	11.5	High
New York	18.1	6.7	14.3	13.0	High
Pennsylvania	13.6	8.9	3.1	10.0	Moderate
Great Lakes					
Illinois	14.6	10.7	3.9	11.0	Moderate
Indiana	10.9	8.5	2.2	7.5	Low
Michigan	12.8	7.7	1.4	9.0	Moderate
Ohio	12.6	9.3	1.9	10.0	Moderate
Wisconsin	10.0	7.4	0.9	6.0	Low
Plains					
Iowa	8.9	10.6	1.0	8.0	Low
Kansas	9.8	8.7	1.8	7.0	Low
Minnesota	9.5	10.5	1.2	8.0	Low
Missouri	14.2	10.9	0.8	11.0	Moderate
Nebraska	10.7	10.4	2.0	8.0	Low
North Dakota	14.2	7.8	1.8	9.0	Moderate
South Dakota	18.5	6.9	1.2	12.0	High
Southeast					
Alabama	21.5	9.4	*	12.0	High
Arkansas	22.2	8.9	*	12.0	High
Florida	16.7	8.6	5.9	13.5	High
Georgia	20.3	9.2	1.0	13.0	High
Kentucky	22.3	9.5	*	12.0	High
Louisiana	23.8	9.9	5.0	14.0	High
Mississippi	31.3	8.5	*	12.0	High
North Carolina	17.4	9.5	*	12.0	High
South Carolina	19.3	11.2	*	13.0	High
Tennessee	21.3	10.6	*	13.0	High
Virginia	13.4	8.5	1.3	10.0	Moderate
West Virginia	17.3	8.5	*	12.0	High

Table 6.2   (Cont.)

State and Region	% Children in Poverty 1980	% Children Served as Handicapped Fall 1979	% Limited-English-Proficient Children Fall 1980	Index of Educational Need	Classification on Educational Need Index
Southwest					
Arizona	14.2	9.3	15.0	11.0	Moderate
New Mexico	21.2	7.2	25.4	13.0	High
Oklahoma	14.4	10.1	2.6	11.0	Moderate
Texas	18.4	8.8	18.0	14.0	High
Rocky Mountain					
Colorado	11.0	7.9	6.3	6.5	Low
Idaho	13.3	8.6	2.7	10.0	Moderate
Montana	12.7	7.8	2.0	9.0	Moderate
Utah	9.7	10.5	2.2	8.0	Low
Wyoming	6.8	9.3	2.1	7.0	Low
Far West					
California	13.8	8.7	14.1	11.0	Moderate
Nevada	9.3	7.3	3.6	6.0	Low
Oregon	10.6	8.4	2.1	7.0	Low
Washington	10.8	6.7	2.2	6.0	Low
Alaska	9.6	9.0	6.7	7.5	Low
Hawaii	11.0	6.2	12.4	7.0	Low

*Not available.
Sources: Prospects for Financing Elementary/Secondary Education in the States, School Finance Project, U.S. Dept. of Education, Vol. I, p. 75; U.S. Department of Commerce, Bureau of the Census, 1980 Census of Population and Housing, *Provisional Estimates of Social, Economic, and Housing Characteristics*, Report #PHC 80-SL, Washington, D.C., March 1982; U.S. Department of HEW, National Center for Educational Statistics, unpublished data; Oxford, Rebecca; Pol Louis; Lopez, David; Stupp, Paul; Peng, Samuel; and Gendell, Murray. *Changes in the Number of Non-English Language Background and Limited English Proficient Persons in the U.S. to the Year 2000: The Projects and How They Were Made.* Roselyn, Va.: Inter-America Research Associates, 1980.

pects tend to be unfavorable. Where the student population is expected to continue to decline or to remain stable funding prospects generally appear favorable. Unfortunately, states that face increasing enrollments and bleak funding prospects also tend to have a relatively high percentage of students who are handicapped, impoverished, or of limited English proficiency (included as part of the index denoted as "Student Need"—see Table 6.3). Worse still, many of these same states lost federal funds due to the changeover to block grants (see Table 6.4). As one can see, the states with unfavorable funding prospects, increased demand for education (i.e., growing student enrollments), and a high proportion of students with special needs received cutbacks in federal funds due to the Education Consolidation and Improvement Act (ECIA). They include Alabama, Georgia, Louisiana, Maine, and Mississippi.

Table 6.3 Characteristics of States Grouped by Funding Prospects

State	Projected Increase in Demand 1985–2000	Student Need 1980	Fiscal Capacity 1981	Education Effort 1980–81	Federal Share of Education Revenues 1980–81	Education Expenditures 1980–81
			Funding Procedures Are Good			
Alaska	MH	L	H*	H	H	H
Connecticut	L	M	H	L	L	H
Delaware	L	M	MH	MH	H	H
D.C.	L	H	H	L	H	H
Illinois	L	M	MH	M	MH	H
Maryland	L	L	H	M	LM	H
Massachusetts	L	M	MH	H	L	H
Michigan	L	M	MH	H	LM	H
Minnesota	M	L	M	H	L	H
New Jersey	L	H	H	MH	L	H
New York	L	H	MH	H	L	H
Oregon	H	L	LM	H	MH	H
Rhode Island	L	M	M	LM	L	H
Washington	MH	L	MH	L	M	H
Wisconsin	LM	L	M	H	L	H
			Funding Procedures Are Average			
Arizona	H	M	LM	H	H	M
California	M**	M	H	L	L	L
Colorado	H	L	MH	H	L	M
Florida	MH	H	M	L	H	M
Hawaii	H	L	MH	L	H	MH
Iowa	M	L	M	MH	L	H
Kansas	MH	L	M	M	L	MH
Missouri	LM	M	LM	L	MH	L
Montana	H	M	LM*	H	M	H
Nebraska	MH	L	M	M	L	M
New Mexico	H	H	L*	H	H	LM
Ohio	L	M	M	M	L	LM
Oklahoma	H	M	M*	M	H	LM
Pennsylvania	L	M	M	MH	L	H
Virginia	LM	M	M	LM	MH	LM
West Virginia	LM	H	L*	H	H	L
Wyoming	H	L	H*	H	L	M
			Funding Procedures Are Unfavorable			
Alabama	MH	H	L	L	H	L
Arkansas	MH	H	L	LM	H	L
Georgia	M	H	L	LM	H	L
Idaho	H	M	L	MH	M	L
Indiana	LM	L	LM	M	L	L
Kentucky	MH	H	L	M	H	L

Table 6.3   (Cont.)

State	Projected Increase in Demand 1985–2000	Student Need 1980	Fiscal Capacity 1981	Education Effort 1980–81	Federal Share of Education Revenues 1980–81	Education Expenditures 1980–81
Louisiana	MH	H	L*	L	H	L
Maine	MH	M	L	H	MH	L
Mississippi	H	H	L	L	H	L
Nevada	H	L	H*	L	L	L
New Hampshire	H	L	M	M	L	L
North Carolina	LM	H	L	LM	H	L
North Dakota	H	M	M*	L	L	L
South Carolina	M	H	L	MH	H	L
South Dakota	H	H	L	LM	H	L
Tennessee	MH	H	L	L	H	L
Texas	H	H	M*	M	H	L
Utah	H	L	L	H	L	L
Vermont	MH	L	L	H	L	L

*States where 1980 index of tax capacity is 10 points or more higher than 1980 income index per capita. On tax capacity Montana, Oklahoma and Texas are classified as H, Louisiana, New Mexico, and North Dakota as MH, and West Virginia as LM.

**California's ranking was reduced from MH to M due to the large increase in private school enrollment.

Source: *Prospects for Financing Elementary/Secondary Education in the States*, School Finance Project, U.S. Dept. of Education, Vol. I, p. vi.

Table 6.4   States' Gains and Losses Under Block Grants

State	1981* Actual Obligations	1982 Continuing Resolution	Percent Change
Alabama	$9,310,777	7,638,238	−17.9
Alaska	1,673,421	2,187,360	+30.7
Arizona	5,713,026	5,101,377	−10.7
Arkansas	4,166,966	4,376,070	+5.0
California	54,246,507	41,310,341	−23.8
Colorado	5,470,881	5,226,034	−4.4
Connecticut	7,705,819	5,629,327	−26.9
Delaware	5,334,320	2,187,360	−58.9
District of Columbia	5,081,817	2,187,360	−56.9
Florida	15,189,568	15,789,102	+3.9
Georgia	12,412,579	10,871,064	−12.4
Hawaii	2,614,896	2,187,360	−16.3
Idaho	2,352,502	2,187,360	−7.0
Illinois	22,001,556	21,174,245	−3.7
Indiana	13,296,399	10,588,588	−20.3
Iowa	5,003,104	5,333,733	+6.6

Table 6.4   (Cont.)

State	1981* Actual Obligations	1982 Continuing Resolution	Percent Change
Kansas	3,998,761	4,131,745	+3.3
Kentucky	5,886,713	7,062,039	+19.9
Louisiana	11,553,890	8,550,185	−25.9
Maine	2,465,710	2,187,360	−11.2
Maryland	7,231,962	7,901,227	+9.2
Massachusetts	10,653,970	10,179,203	−4.4
Michigan	20,542,592	18,242,264	−11.2
Minnesota	6,610,381	7,634,133	+15.4
Mississipi	7,674,512	5,286,720	−31.1
Missouri	17,567,404	8,900,251	−49.3
Montana	2,444,590	2,187,360	−10.5
Nebraska	3,728,418	2,862,882	−23.2
Nevada	1,700,010	2,187,360	+28.6
New Hampshire	2,117,783	2,187,360	+3.2
New Jersey	15,530,875	13,483,247	−13.2
New Mexico	3,514,388	2,666,637	−24.1
New York	48,291,827	31,353,236	−35.0
North Carolina	10,689,571	11,053,883	−3.4
North Dakota	1,951,219	2,187,360	+12.1
Ohio	25,208,194	20,366,440	−19.2
Oklahoma	5,085,337	5,487,749	+7.9
Oregon	4,296,691	4,634,193	+7.8
Pennsylvania	20,340,163	20,977,320	+3.1
Rhode Island	2,807,257	2,187,360	−22.0
South Carolina	6,436,972	6,207,221	−3.5
South Dakota	2,003,848	2,187,360	+9.1
Tennessee	7,862,551	8,583,914	−9.2
Texas	27,272,790	27,688,367	+1.5
Utah	3,003,797	3,090,754	+2.8
Vermont	1,809,738	2,187,360	−20.9
Virginia	11,701,345	9,830,541	−16.0
Washington	9,658,260	7,352,566	−23.8
West Virginia	3,282,349	3,654,895	+11.3
Wisconsin	13,788,358	8,923,105	−35.2
Wyoming	1,743,256	2,187,360	+25.4

*Data were obtained from reports of actual obligations by state for the 29 antecedent programs consolidated into the block grant.

Source: Editorial Projects in Education. *The American Education Deskbook 1982–83*, Washington, D.C., 1982, p. 158.

Those who advocated consolidation or "block grants" claimed that while federal funding would be reduced by 25 percent, the actual loss of revenues would amount to only 12 percent, as the savings accrued from reduced paperwork would reach 13 percent. Henry Levin has stated that such estimates were overly optimistic and that the actual savings would only, on average, total 4 percent (1981).

In addition to conflicts that stem from cuts in overall levels of funding, some predict that a reduced level of federal involvement might heighten state and local conflict due to a shift in special interest group lobbying efforts from the federal level to state and local levels.

Political Trends

As stated earlier, some scholars of educational politics believe that with the 1980 presidential election came the beginning of a new politics of education. Iannaccone has written that:

> The present educational situation in national politics is markedly different from previous realignment elections. National education policies and the educational policymaking function of national government were an important feature of the 1980 campaigns. A change in that function is a salient part of the challenge the Reagan administration makes to the policy premises of the previous quarter century (1982, p. 6).

However, Iannaccone good naturedly warns us that he has been predicting "a revolution ahead in the politics and governance of education" since 1966 (1982, p. 7).

The present authors feel that it is too soon to judge whether or not the revolution has begun, or ever will begin. The Department of Education still stands, vouchers have not become a reality, and the number of students in private schools has not greatly increased since Reagan's inauguration. Still, it is possible that great change might occur, though not necessarily in the direction intended by the present administration. The National Commission on Excellence in Education's report, *A Nation at Risk* (1983), has put education back on the front page of the news. If schools are to be "reformed" and teacher salaries to be increased, some branch of government will have to foot the bill, but which branch is not yet clear. While state financing of education and involvement in educational policy making have increased substantially over the past decade, competition from other sources for funds from the state coffers is likely to thwart any attempts to increase state aid for education in the near future.

The overwhelming majority of superintendents in our study reported that state and federal regulations caused problems for them. In many ways the two types of interventions are related, as the funds provided by the federal government made it possible for state departments of education to increase their capacities to regulate local districts. Jerome Murphy notes that many state education agencies have doubled or tripled in size since the mid-1960s (1982, p. 199). A recent study entitled "The Interaction of Federal and Related State Education Programs" estimated that *half* of the staff in state education agencies were supported with federal funds (Moore et al. 1983). It is unclear what role the state would play if federal regulations in certain areas were to change. For example, respondents from state and local education agencies predicted that "if federal protections for handicapped education were removed, . . . state laws would follow suit" (Moore et al. 1983, p. 8).

Moore and others found that due to "the heavy federal subsidization of staff in federal programs, state officials did not, by and large, complain about the administrative burdens imposed by federal programs" (p. 10). In a similar manner, while superintendents might complain about state and federal programs, administrative coordinators and teachers in these special projects are likely to support the existence of the state and federal presence. Elmore and McLaughlin have referred to these loyalties to state and federal sources as vertical, as opposed to horizontal, networks. They caution that the two types of networks within one school system may sometimes act at cross-purposes and conflict and inefficiencies may be likely byproducts (1982).

Murphy makes the point that as federal involvement has strengthened the role of state education agencies, they in turn increase the power of local education agencies "because at both levels there are a lot more issues and programs to be influenced by a lot more people" (1982, p. 207). He adds to this an interesting explanation for the frequency with which school superintendents complain about state regulations:

By providing local districts with the resources to implement state mandates, state action has also unintentionally strengthened countervailing local forces. The resources have been used to build local professional staffs who demand more, who are more sophisticated about state-local relations, who resist orders, and who are more willing and able to complain loudly about how the states are operating. Moreover, the growth in local power helps explain the seemingly contradictory behavior of critics who complain about state regulations yet seek additional state intervention. Often, state action increases not only state power but local power as well, and local officials have been willing—while complaining—to trade off some local autonomy for an expansion of local influence (p. 207).

But what happens when state and federal programs, or funding levels, are cut back? Do local school officials effectively fight back to protect their recent expansion of influence? So far, school administrators do not seem to have mounted a strong campaign to maintain or increase federal spending for public schools. While "political action committees" have been formed by AFT, NEA, and noneducators concerned with budget cuts in the field of education, school administrators as a group seem reluctant to do so. Joseph Scherer, AASA associate executive director in charge of governmental relations, explains why:

Superintendents are politicians in order to survive, but they're not elected and what they represent is considered "pure." People were always supposed to support education, but we're finding that just isn't true (Rudensky 1982).

It is difficult to predict whether or not recent elimination of requirements for parent or public involvement as advisors in federal programs will affect lobbying for support for public schools. Advisory councils are no longer required at the local level for Title I, Migrant Education, Emergency School Aid, School Improvement, and Ethnic Heritage Studies as of September 30, 1982, because of the Education Consolidation and Improvement Act. This might increase lobbying at the state and local levels if these citizens no longer feel their voices are heard at the federal level. It is equally plausible that when such advisory councils are no longer in place, the pursuit of the goals sought by such groups loses momentum.

While some superintendents feel that advisory groups increase the time they must spend in conflict resolution, others feel that such groups, when used effectively enhance their lobbying power for additional federal funds and help to minimize conflict at the local level. Steele et al. have revealed that "superintendents can nurture special interest groups to the point where some interest groups become institutionalized so that they can become buffers to attacks and incursions from other interest groups and the public in general" (1981, p. 268). One would expect, therefore, that the degree to which superintendents will fight both cutbacks in federal funding and the "strings" that accompany such funding depends on the degree to which they have felt truly restricted by federal regulations.

At the federal level, which provides only approximately 8 percent of the total revenues supporting schools, the question seems to be whether educators feel it is worth the trouble to rebuild tattered alliances. Albert Shanker, president of the AFT, recently commented that teachers should give the concept of merit pay some consideration. This suggests that some educators are willing to take unprecedented steps to encourage greater financial support for public school teachers (and perhaps even education), though the source of increased revenues to attract higher quality teachers is as yet undetermined.

At the state level the question seems to be whether educators *can* rebuild tattered alliances. Kirst and Somers (1980) and Elmore and McLaughlin (1982) have chronicled the efforts of educators in California who strove to maintain funding levels for public schools in the wake of Proposition 13. While the efforts were generally successful, differences over strategies between some proeducation lobbyists known as the Tuesday Night Group and members of the Association of California School Administrators weakened the strength of the coalition and created delays in the legislative process. What is clear from this experience is that it is far more difficult to maintain coalitions when the pie is shrinking rather than expanding. Therefore, whether or not educators will be able to collectively and effectively lobby for greater resources depends largely on the overall economy and general public opinion about whether or not education's share of the public purse should be increased. Recent national attention to the fact that the technological sectors of the economy are rapidly expanding, and concern about whether students are receiving the skills needed to meet future job demands suggests that support for and interest in education may be building to a peak, the likes of which we have not seen since the Sputnik era.

What Have We Learned?

One of the aims of this study was to resolve the apparent contradiction between research that indicates that superintendents, rather than lay boards, dominate educational decision making (Zeigler, Jennings, and Peak 1974; Peterson 1974; Tucker and Zeigler 1980) and the assertion that superintendents are beleaguered (McCarty and Ramsey 1971; Maeroff 1975). When one attempts to address the question, "Are superintendents beleaguered?" it makes sense to ask also, "Relative to whom?" In this study, the role of the superintendent in educational governance is compared to that of the city manager in municipal governance because of their similarities: both are managers of local politics shaped by the reform movement; both are selected by and legally accountable to lay boards or councils; and both face similar conflict issues such as those related to finance, state and federal regulation, and collective bargaining.

When one compares superintendents to city managers the data seem to refute the beleaguered superintendent hypothesis. Superintendents spend significantly less time overall managing conflict than do city managers. Superintendents also spend substantially less time resolving conflict with their legislative bodies than do city managers. Likewise, superintendents report low levels of disagreement among the public significantly more often than do city managers. Also, when the public does get involved in conflicts regarding school matters, they tend to participate as individuals rather than as members of groups. The opposite is true for municipal matters. Furthermore, when groups did form to influence educational issues, they were more likely to be internal to the school district than the counterpart groups in municipal governance. In California, where both school districts and municipalities are facing cutbacks in resources and personnel, city managers report higher levels of conflict between themselves and the administrative staff and line officers than do superintendents. In addition, city managers generally spend more time with state and federal agencies attempting to manage conflict than do superintendents. All this suggests that superintendents are not beleaguered when compared to their counterparts in local government.

Another plausible response to the question of superintendents' relative state of beleaguerment is, "Compared to when?" Over the past two decades both superintendents and city managers have witnessed increased levels of state and federal involvement, a higher incidence of collective bargaining, greater concern over equity issues, and changes in educational and municipal finance. In addition, increasingly scarce resources make conflict management skills an ever more important part of the job of public administrators. If one accepts the hypothesis that superintendents' professional training tends to confirm a view of conflict that is negative, then one might expect superintendents to report more tension as a result of conflict-laden changes than do city managers.

In fact, when one looks at the data on specific issues, superintendents report that finances, collective bargaining, and federal intervention are problem areas substantially more often than do city managers. However, these issues may create more problems for superintendents because of the nature of the issues involved. School districts may suffer budget cuts due to declining enrollments in addition to suffering constraints from financial factors that also affect municipalities. The scope of bargaining may be more difficult to delineate in the educational than in the municipal sphere and therefore the level of conflict may be greater. Furthermore, a higher level of federal involvement in educational policy making may account for the fact that superintendents named federal intervention as a source of problems more often than did city managers.

In addition, though, the fact that superintendents report a greater number of problem areas, yet spend less time managing conflict, may be attributable to the fact that they are less likely than city managers to view conflict management as an essential part of their jobs and consequently may have a greater tendency to avoid it. A greater number of superintendents than city managers indicated that they would not take a stand of which either the board/council or the public disapproved. Similarly, almost half of all superintendents interviewed reported that they had not made any policy recommendation that was rejected by the board. (A number of them stated that they did not make a recommendation unless they felt reasonably sure it would be supported by the board.) In contrast, all but a few city managers had made policy recommendations that were later turned down. This evidence suggests that superintendents seem less willing to enter into situations that may generate conflict, perhaps because they have been relatively sheltered from conflict until fairly recently.

One city manager offered the following insight about the relative changes in the jobs of superintendents and city managers over the past two decades:

> I, and I think other city managers, used to be jealous of superintendents until about 1965. They were referred to as "Dr." (when we felt our master's programs were as difficult or more difficult). They got paid more, and they had less conflict because people were more deferential to them. They also had less work in the summer and had contracts which city managers didn't have. Since the late sixties, however, the two groups have become more similar. The superintendents joined "the real world of conflict." Average salaries of the two groups approached each other, and superintendents have become less secure in their positions due to higher turnover, while a greater number of city managers have been given contracts.

The change in the role of the superintendent was also succinctly described by the superintendent in the same locality:

> The job of superintendent has changed radically over the past twenty years. When I started as superintendent I came in with an orientation that I wanted to help people and be liked. But over time I have undergone a difficult personal transformation by learning to accept conflict as the reality of the job. Now I have to deal with teacher militancy, closing schools, firing teachers, being more accountable for costs, and working with more active parents and citizens.

At a 1981 conference, Kenneth Duckworth described the tensions of school administrators as stemming from a conflict between the job roles of "heroes" versus "heralds." He referred to the definition of hero as "a mythological or legendary figure often of divine descent endowed with great strength or ability" and suggested that it was this type of idealism or ideology that might encourage people to enter into the field of school administration or instructional leadership. The comment by the superintendent wanting "to help people and be liked" illustrates this idealism. Yet, due to the increased political nature of the job, superintendents are more frequently called on to play the role of heralds, which is defined as "an official at a tournament of arms with duties including the making of announcements and the marshalling of combatants" (Duckworth 1981). Both of these symbolic images exemplify the alterations in the role of the superintendency over time; having one's job description changed from hero to herald may be grounds for claiming "beleaguerment."

The number of differences between superintendents and city managers leads us to conclude that there is more to account for in the school control over decision making than the nature of the issue, as suggested by Boyd. As discussed earlier, we believe the professional training of school superintendents encourages them to dominate lay boards and to minimize conflict. As previously described, school superintendents advocated taking an active role in policy making and even in board elections significantly more than did city managers. Presumably, the superintendents' goal was to minimize conflict that might come as a result of true lay participation. At any rate, they seem to face lower levels of conflict from both the public and their school boards than their counterparts in municipal government. Those who train school administrators have for a long while claimed that politics have no legitimate role in the educational arena. John Dewey, for example, stated in *The Public and Its Problems* that questions regarding curriculum, selection of personnel, and management of finances should be resolved by experts.

> These are technical matters, as much as the construction of an efficient engine, to be settled by inquiry into facts; and as the inquiry can be carried on only by those especially equipped, so the results of inquiry can be utilized only by trained technicians. What has the counting of heads, decisions by majority, and the whole apparatus of traditional government to do with such things (1954, p. 125)?

More recently, many school administrators have come to accept the fact that their job is a political one. One former school superintendent recently wrote, "If we intend to retain power, we must master the skills of the more politicized styles of city managers" (Apker 1982, p. 15). Now that competition for resources has stiffened due to declining enrollments, other social priorities, and a

failing economy, school administrators need to become effective lobbyists. Apker, now executive director of the Colorado Association of
School Executives, has also commented that "except for the largest
school districts, which by statute or disdain, operate in an expanded
zone of indifference outside the jurisdiction of state departments, or
which lobby directly, we administrators have remained remarkably
aloof from the state political process" (1982, p. 15). As noted earlier,
whether enrollments increase or decrease, superintendents need to
be aware of how demographics alter the need for resources in their
districts. Also, knowledge of financial and political trends will enhance their ability to make sure the resources needed are secured.
Perhaps one of the toughest groups to convince to support public
schools is local property owners who want their tax burdens reduced. Many school districts have begun to use new methods of
budgeting such as school-site budgeting, zero-base budgeting, and
program-oriented budgeting so that local taxpayers can see the con-
nection between revenues collected and what is allocated to actual
schools or programs. School districts hope that taxpayers will see
that schools can be held accountable and will consequently increase
(or at least maintain) their support.

    To our surprise, we also learned that superintendents do use
political methods to resolve conflicts, even slightly more often than
do city managers (though the difference is not significant). In addition, both superintendents and city managers vary their styles depending on whether the conflict is contained within the organization
or not. If the conflict involves people outside of the district or municipal government, both groups of administrators tend to use political
conflict management behaviors rather than those that we have classified as "technocratic."

    The average tenure rates of superintendents and city man-
agers in our sample were remarkably similar. Interestingly, as the
number of years spent in their present positions increased, both
superintendents and managers experienced a significant drop in the
amount of time they spent in conflict management. This was also
true for the relationship between age and years of administrative
experience and time spent managing conflict. Also, the greater the
administrative experience the less time these public sector executives spent in conflict with their boards or councils. In addition, the
number of years of experience in their present positions was significantly negatively related to the level of conflict in their communi-

ties. This last phenomenon might be explained either by the fact that administrators become more effective in managing conflict in their communities over time or, perhaps, that those with many years in one position survived for so long because of the low level of conflict inherent in their communities.

It is extremely difficult to say how superintendents and city managers (or those aspiring to these positions) might improve their conflict management skills. Perhaps through managing conflict on the job, administrators become more effective conflict managers and consequently spend less time at it. On the other hand, time spent in conflict management may cause burnout. Caldwell and Forney report from their survey of over 150 Pennsylvania school administrators that administrators "tended to view their school system as less 'open' and less 'participative' as their reported age, years in administration, and years in their present position increased" (1982, p. 10). This suggests that perhaps school superintendents spend less time in conflict as age, years in administration, and years in their present position increased because they have lost some hope and idealism.

James Enochs, assistant superintendent for the Modesto Schools, states that the field of education is seriously in need of stronger leaders:

> Let's face it, there is something wrong with a profession in which the two most popular workshops for the putative leaders of the profession are stress management and planning for early retirement. It does not inspire confidence to see administrators spending their time preparing for breakdown or escape. And *confidence is the most important currency of leadership* (1981, p. 177).

He also states that education needs leaders unafraid to take risks. This might be asking a lot of a profession where a large proportion entered as teachers in search of job security and where policy recommendations to the school board are not made until they are virtually assured of acceptance.

Recently, interest in the virtues of leadership over management has grown. Levinson writes:

> Leadership transcends and subsumes management. Leaders these days deal with conflicting forces of multiple constituen-

cies outside the organization and similarly conflicting forces within the organization. Organizations cannot readily adopt without internal conflicting forces, since these enable people to examine the multifaceted nature of problems and their possible solutions. Organizations without loyal opposition become stultified bureaucracies; without external opposition they are unable to realize their contributions to society as a whole (Rost 1982).

Perhaps, as Levinson suggests, due to experience in conflict management stemming from changing demographic, financial, and political conditions, school administrators will expand the scope of their search for solutions.

Responsiveness Revisited

Our data suggest that school districts tend to be more removed from conflict and public demands than municipalities. School boards appear to operate with a much higher level of consensus than do city councils. The findings indicate that not only is there a significantly lower level of disagreement among boards than councils, but that the board is substantially more likely to be in agreement with the superintendent over the appropriate role of the chief executive officer than is the council with the city manager. It is also substantially less likely that there will be a disagreement between the chief executive officer and the legislative body in school districts than in municipalities, as examined earlier. To reiterate, an earlier study of school governance reported that when a superintendent's position on an issue is known, he or she is successful in having the position accepted in approximately 99 percent of all cases (Tucker and Zeigler 1980, p. 144). Almost half of the superintendents included in our sample stated that none of their policy recommendations had been rejected by the school board. Very few managers made this claim concerning their recommendations to the city council.

The public appears to participate less in decisions within the educational policy-making sphere. The number of citizens' committees connected with school boards was significantly lower than those working with city councils. When the public does become informally involved in school conflicts, they generally participate as individuals rather than as members of groups. Furthermore, as stated earlier, when groups do form to influence educational issues, they are more likely to be internal to the school district.

Decreased responsiveness to the public may result, in part, from board members being chosen at elections that are at-large, nonpartisan, and held separately from other elections, a major result of the reform movement. Anne Just aptly summarizes the effects of these measures as follows:

> These conditions (1) kept voter turnout low and restricted to those directly affected by the election—teachers and parents of students; (2) depressed levels of competition, apparently by scaring away potential candidates; (3) discouraged the rejection of incumbents standing for reelection; and (4) diminished the exposition of differences among candidates (1980, p. 425).

According to the extensive data collected by Zeigler, Jennings, and Peak, the impact of the reform movement on reducing competition for school board seats (measured in three ways: presence of opposition for the primary or election, office turnover, and incumbent defeat) is strongly felt in metropolitan areas (1974, pp. 57–59). One reason for this is the larger effort required to campaign for a seat on the board of an urban district. The lower level of school board turnover in metropolitan areas may also be seen as a symptom of a less-than-responsive electorate. Consequently, since the turn of the century, school board members not only represent a greater number of citizens, but also may be even less responsive to their needs, especially in the cities.

In addition to structural changes that inhibit the likelihood that the public will become involved in school affairs, another factor diminishes the probability that even those who do participate by attending board meetings will have any affect on board policy. Lutz suggests that there are generally agreed-upon norms at board meetings that limit participation in the decision-making process. He states:

> School boards strive for consensus among themselves. They think of themselves as trustees for the people, not delegates of the people. They usually arrive at decisions by consensus reached in private "work sessions." They come to public board meetings armed with the previous consensus to enact that decision by unanimous vote. The superintendent, who usually has actively participated in the formulation of the decision, carries out the decision. If in the public meeting there is any dissension or the consensus begins to fall apart, the issue is most often referred to committee "for further study" in order to reestablish a consensus. Is it any wonder that some groups feel disenfranchised, unrepresented, or governed by others, and that these

decisions favor the interests of these others? Is it any wonder
that those groups do not support public schools or work to improve them (1980, pp. 460–61)?

The evidence suggests that neither the school board nor the
public is as actively involved in educational policy making as their
counterparts in municipalities. This lack of involvement may cause
the superintendent to become less responsive to lay demands.
While the electorate could, in fact, replace school board members
with those who would hire a more responsive superintendent, our
data suggest that this occurs much less commonly in school districts than in municipalities. Not only is turnover much lower for
school boards than city councils, but the number of citizens even
interested in running for the school board is substantially lower than
those running for the city council. While it is difficult to collect accurate data explaining the circumstances of superintendents' or city
managers' terminations (since they may have left for another job
knowing that their contracts would not be renewed), superintendents were shown to be significantly less likely than city managers
to leave their positions for reasons other than retirement. This may
suggest that school boards are less likely than city councils to pressure their chief executives into leaving. All in all, the data we collected recently in over 50 districts and municipalities in the Chicago
and San Francisco metropolitan areas indicate no resurgence of
school board power or responsiveness to the public. Cistone and Iannaccone recently wrote that "for the second time in a century, we
are experiencing a revolution in the politics of education, one that
appears likely to lead to a revolutionary change in the character of
educational governance" (1980, p. 419). While a number of changes
in political, economic, and demographic conditions have recently occurred, the effects of revolution in school governance have not yet
made themselves readily apparent according to our recent research.
       Not all those who have examined the arena of educational pol-
icy making would conclude that schools are essentially dominated
by professionals and are unresponsive to the public. Frank Lutz, for
example, has recently argued to the contrary.

> First, local school boards *are* a fundamental grassroots unit of
> democracy in the United States. Second, in spite of declarations
> to the contrary, local school boards largely retain the effective
> control of education in the United States (1980, p. 452).

However, the previous statement by Lutz suggests that he, too, is not thoroughly convinced that school boards are truly democratic. Still others suggest that while the thesis presented by Zeigler, Jennings, and Peak reflects school governance in the previous decade, it is no longer accurate today since public involvement has purportedly increased with the advent of federally mandated parent advisory groups. In addition, Just has commented that school districts may have recently become more responsive to citizen or parent involvement due to federal programs for minorities and the disadvantaged and to the mandated advisory committees that form a part of these programs. She also noted that Zeigler, Jennings, and Peak's conclusion may not be generalizable to large cities, as various changes have occurred in urban school districts that "the study probably would not capture" (Just 1980, p. 430). Recent research, it turns out, does not support either of these criticisms. Gittell and her associates examined 16 community organizations in Boston, Atlanta, and Los Angeles, including parent advisory councils for Title I, and found little evidence of an actual increase in lay participation in the educational policy-making process. Their findings have been summarized as follows:

> Not only were they surprised to find "no school-issue-oriented, self-initiated, lower-income organization in any of three cities" but they also found that the dependency of the organizations they studied on external or school system sources precluded the use of advocacy strategies in pursuit of educational reform. In effect, these organizations appeared to be "toothless tigers" (Boyd and Crowson 1981, p. 356).

An earlier case study of a community school movement in an urban district likewise confirmed the thesis that educational policy making is dominated by the professionals, even when the lay public is formally involved (Boyd and Seldin 1975).

Still others caution that even though the public may not actively participate in school policy making, this failure may not afford ample evidence for concluding as did Zeigler, Jennings, and Peak, that school boards are unresponsive or undemocratic. Lutz points out that "American democracy was never envisioned as a direct democracy, but as a representative democracy. The essence of democracy is freedom to participate (or not to participate)" (1980, p. 454). He argues that citizens tend not to participate unless they are dissatisfied, or in other words, unless the actions taken by the schools fall outside the citizens' conception of an acceptable "zone of tolerance." If members of the local community do become dissatisfied, he predicts an increase in the challengers to incumbents in school board elections, the total voter turnout, and the percentage of votes cast for the nonincumbents (p. 456). Then, according to the dissatisfaction theory proposed by Iannaccone and Lutz (1970), school board incumbents are more likely to be defeated over the next few elections and the superintendent may eventually be replaced. While a recent study has empirically verified that there are episodic periods of incumbent defeats (generally lasting for three election periods), followed by relatively calm periods (Criswell and Mitchell 1980), the researchers note that more evidence is needed to demonstrate that these defeats arise from actual disagreement with, or loss of support for, board policy or school district operations before the dissatisfaction theory can be substantiated.

Even if the dissatisfaction theory were verified, it does not necessarily hold that school policy and operations would necessarily change to better reflect community preferences. Criswell and Mitchell begin to address this problem:

> According to the Iannaccone-Lutz theory, a mandate for substantial policy change is triggered by the election of an insurgent school board member and must be passed on to the school manager. This mandate for change all too often takes the form of a dismissal of the school manager (p. 210).

This statement implies that dismissal of the superintendent may diminish the effective implementation of the new school board's mandate. However, in another article Mitchell suggests that it is precisely the school board's involvement in the recruitment and hiring of a new superintendent who will carry out their ideological "mandate" that allows them to "exercise their control over school operations" (1980, p. 447). (Actually Mitchell states that Carlson [1972] has reached these conclusions, but this does not seem wholly accurate.) He refers to Carlson's study (1972) *School Superintendents: Careers and Performance* to give credence to his argument:

> Carlson noted that if school boards wish to have existing programs stabilized and maintained, they will promote an "insider" to the superintendency, while a mandate for innovation and

change will lead to the hiring of an "outsider" brought into the
district for the explicit purpose of initiating program change
(1980, p. 447).

As a matter of fact, Carlson's research (1972) also indicates that the
superintendents were hired for generally broad reasons. While
superintendents hired from the "outside" (i.e., those who are career-bound) rather than from the "inside" (i.e., those who are place-
bound) significantly more often stated that they had been selected
by the school board because of "improvement desired," it seems
that the "mandate for change" they received included a high degree
of discretion over the control of school operations. Carlson describes
the situation as follows:

> By taking someone from outside the containing organization
> and giving him a mandate, the board signals a desire for a break
> with old ways. In this sense the board commits itself. Thus it
> must go with the career-bound man and give him the backing
> needed to carry out the mandate. More than one school board
> president has said that he viewed his *sole* function the first year
> as that of supporting the new man (p. 84).

Thus, it does not appear that in the board's recruitment of the superintendent it is exercising "control over school operations."

In a similar manner, it is difficult to assess whether or not individual citizens or special interest groups affect school operations or
policy making merely because they are active. Tucker and Zeigler's
research suggests that school officials are not generally responsive
to publicly expressed demands (1980). It also implies that it is difficult to adequately measure responsiveness. For example, a school
board's or administrator's failure to respond to citizens' demands
may be attributable to the fact that no dominant lay position could
be discerned or that more information was needed prior to making a
decision, rather than to a general lack of responsiveness. Tucker
and Zeigler point out that the school board makes a decision in response to publicly expressed demands in less than 4 percent of all
school discussions (1980, p. 215).

Despite this apparent lack of responsiveness, Salisbury's study
of citizen participation in the public schools reveals that, of those
who participate in school-related activities, "75 percent of the respondents believe that their participation has had an impact on the

schools, 90 percent think that schools will be responsive to their concerns, and 92 percent think that they can influence school decisions" (Firestone 1981, p. 219). Moreover, 83 percent of the participants, compared to 60 percent of the general public, approve of the schools' performances. Salisbury's findings suggest that if school administrators did allow for greater public participation, although such participation would test their conflict management skills, public support for local schools might be strengthened.

Conclusion

Now that the Reagan administration is seeking to minimize the federal role in schooling and to strengthen the role of the local and state governments in educational policy making, it seems all the more imperative to reestablish school boards as a viable and responsive institution. A few scholars have recently indicated that there may be an increase in the level of politicization in school board elections, especially in the larger cities, though no concrete data are evident. For example, Just and Guthrie have recently cited each other as having written that school board candidates are increasingly getting endorsements from local and state officials (Guthrie 1981, p. 70; Just 1980, p. 432). At any rate, many politicians and educators have recently stated that New York City district school board campaigns have become increasingly political since the beginning of the past decade. Arlene Pedone, an assistant to former Schools Chancellor Frank J. Macciarola, summarized this viewpoint as follows:

> For a few years, the politicians left the school boards alone, but now that money is tight all over, they're coming back (*New York Times*, March 15, 1983, p. 84).

Since a period of declining resources in education is likely to continue throughout the 1980s, school boards that become more political may be better able to react to the conflicts that will likely ensue. At least one urban school district recently decided to reinstate partisan elections because it was felt that a greater number of interested candidates would emerge if political parties were involved to support the campaigning process. Without partisan elections, it tends to be the professional educators who have a vested interest in school board and bond elections and who are actively campaigning and encouraging citizens sympathetic to their cause to vote.*

Local voters have become less willing to approve an increase in school budgets than was true during the previous period of increasing enrollments. Also, other social service functions previously handled at the federal level are being shifted to the local and state levels. Public schools may also soon face greater competition from private schools due to vouchers or tuition tax-credit plans. A number of observers fear that conflict in school districts will rise sharply as competition for resources mounts. In the future, if they wish to maintain present levels of financial support, school board members and school administrators will need to make a concerted effort to build a stronger case for the public schools both within and outside of their own ranks. In addition, if school officials are going to maintain their credibility with the public as they are faced with conflicting demands and budget reductions, they must learn not only to be more responsive, but also to effectively manage conflict.

---

*We are grateful to Jane Arends, of the Center for Educational Policy and Management, for giving us this insight.

APPENDIXES

—APPENDIX A—
Professional Attitude Scale Items

	Very Well	Well	Neutral	Poorly	Very Poorly
1. My fellow professionals have a pretty good idea about others' competence.	<u>VW</u>	W	?	P	VP
2. I don't have much opportunity to exercise my own judgment.	VW	W	?	P	<u>VP</u>
3. I believe that the professional organization(s) should be supported.	<u>VW</u>	W	?	P	VP
4. Some other occupations are actually more important to society than mine is.	VW	W	?	P	<u>VP</u>
5. The professional organization doesn't really do too much for the average member.	VW	W	?	P	<u>VP</u>
6. We really have no way of judging each other's competence.	VW	W	?	P	<u>VP</u>
7. Although I would like to, I really don't read the journals too often.	VW	W	?	P	<u>VP</u>
8. Most people would stay in the profession even if their incomes were reduced.	<u>VW</u>	W	?	P	VP
9. My own decisions are subject to review.	VW	W	?	P	<u>VP</u>
10. There is not much opportunity to judge how another person does his/her work.	VW	W	?	P	<u>VP</u>

	Very Well	Well	Neutral	Poorly	Very Poorly
11. There are very few people who don't really believe in their work.	VW	W	?	P	VP

The underlined responses reflect the strongest professional attitude.

—APPENDIX B—
Leadership Role Scale Items

1. A city manager should advocate major changes in city policies.
   <u>X</u> strongly agree   ___tend to agree
   ___tend to disagree   ___strongly disagree
2. A city manager should give a helping hand to good councilmen who are coming up for reelection.
   <u>X</u> strongly agree   ___tend to agree
   ___tend to disagree   ___strongly disagree
3. A city manager should maintain a neutral stand on any issues on which the community is divided.
   ___strongly agree   ___tend to agree
   ___tend to disagree   <u>X</u> strongly disagree
4. A city manager should offer the board an opinion only when his/her opinion is requested.
   ___strongly agree   ___tend to agree
   ___tend to disagree   <u>X</u> strongly disagree
5. A city manager should assume leadership in shaping municipal policies.
   <u>X</u> strongly agree   ___tend to agree
   ___tend to disagree   ___strongly disagree
6. A city manager should encourage people whom he/she respects to run for the city council.
   <u>X</u> strongly agree   ___tend to agree
   ___tend to disagree   ___strongly disagree
7. A city manager should act as an administrator and leave policy matters to the council.
   ___strongly agree   ___tend to agree
   ___tend to disagree   <u>X</u> strongly disagree
8. A city manager should advocate policies to which important parts of the community may be hostile.
   <u>X</u> strongly agree   ___tend to agree
   ___tend to disagree   ___strongly disagree

"X" indicates responses that reflect the strongest leadership role. Also, please note that an identical version of these questions was administered to school superintendents using school superintendents as the reference group.

BIBLIOGRAPHY

Bibliography

Agger, Robert; Goldrich, Daniel; and Swanson, Bert. 1964. *The Rulers and the Ruled*. New York: John Wiley.

Ambach, Gordon. 1983. Comments at a meeting of The New York State Board of Regents Advisory Council to The Regents New York City Project at New York City on June 23.

American Association of School Administrators. 1982. "AASA Opinions and Status Survey." *The School Administrator* (September): 32–33.

Anderson, Barry D., and Mark, Jonathan H. 1983. "Declining Revenues and Personnel Allocation in School Districts." Paper presented at the annual meeting of the American Educational Research Association, April 1983 in Montreal, Canada.

———. 1977. "Teacher Mobility and Production in a Metropolitan Area: A Seven Year Study." *Urban Education* 12 (April): 15–36.

Apker, Wesley. 1982. "Building Power Relationships." *The School Administrator* (September): 14–15.

Aufderheide, J. Alan. 1974. "Educational Interest Groups and the State Legislature." In *State Policy Making for the Public Schools*, edited by Ronald Campbell and Tim Mazzoni. Columbus, Ohio: Ohio State University.

Bailey, Stephen K. 1971. "Preparing Administrators for Conflict Resolution." *Educational Record* 52 (Summer): 233–39.

Banfield, Edward C., and Wilson, James Q. 1966. *City Politics*. 2nd edition. New York: Random House.

———. 1963. *City Politics*. New York: Vintage.

Barnard, Chester I. 1958. *The Functions of the Executive*. Cambridge, Mass.: Harvard University Press.

Baron, George, and Tropp, Asher. 1961. "Teachers in England and America." In *Education, Economy, and Society*, edited by Jean Floud and C. Arnold Anderson. New York: The Free Press.

Benveniste, Guy. 1977. *The Politics of Expertise*. San Francisco: Boyd and Fraser.

175

Blake, Robert R., and Mouton, Jane S. 1961. *Group Dynamics: Key to Decisionmaking*. Houston: Gulf Publishing Company.

Blau, Peter M., and Scott, W. Richard. 1962. *Formal Organizations*. San Francisco: Chandler.

Boss, Michael O., and Zeigler, Harmon. 1977. "Experts and Representatives Comparative Bases of Influence in Educational Policy-Making." *Western Political Quarterly* (June): 259.

Boss, Michael O.; Zeigler, Harmon; Tucker, Harvey; and Wilson, L. A., II. 1976. "Professionalism, Community Structure, and Decision-making: School Superintendents and Interest Groups." *Policy Studies Journal* 4 (Summer): 351–62.

Boudon, Raymond. 1973. *Education, Opportunity and Social Inequality*. New York: John Wiley.

Boulding, Kenneth E. 1962. *Conflict and Defense*. New York: Harper.

Boyd, William L. 1982a. "The Politics of Declining Enrollments and School Closings." In *The Changing Politics of School Finance*, edited by Nelda H. Bambron-McCabe and Allan Odden. Cambridge, Mass.: Ballinger.

———. 1982b. "The Politics of School Closings in Ten U.S. Cities." Paper presented at annual meeting of the American Educational Research Association, March 20, 1982, in New York.

———. 1979. "Educational Policy-Making in Declining Suburban School Districts: Some Preliminary Findings." *Education and Urban Society* 11 (May): 333–66.

———. 1976a. "Community Status and Conflict in Suburban School Politics." *Sage Professional Papers in American Politics* 4 [.025] Sage: Beverly Hills, CA.

———. 1976b. "The Public, The Professionals, and Educational Policy-Making: Who Governs." *Teachers College Record* 77: 539–77.

———. 1975. "School Board-Administrative Staff Relationships." In *Understanding School Boards*, edited by Peter Cistone. Lexington, Mass.: Lexington Books.

Boyd, William L., and Crowson, Robert L. 1981. "The Changing Conception and Practice of Public School Administration." In *Review of Educational Research* 9, edited by David Berliner, pp. 311, 73. Washington, D.C.: American Educational Research Association.

Boyd, William L., and Seldin, Florence. 1975. "The Politics of School Reform in Rochester, New York." *Educational and Urban Society* 7: 439–63.

Boynton, Robert P. 1976. "City Councils: Their Role in the Legislative System." In *The Municipal Year Book*. Washington, D.C.: International City Management Association.

Brown, Julius S. 1970. "Risk Propensity in Decision Making: A Comparison of Business and Public School Administrators." *Administrative Science Quarterly* 15 (December): 473–81.

Burns, James McGregor. 1978. *Leadership*. New York: Harper & Row.

Caldwell, Peggy. 1982. "States' Experts Oppose Key Competency-Testing Practices." *Education Week* (January 19): 6–7.

Caldwell, William E., and Forney, Janet W. 1982. "The Relationship of Role Conflict and Ambiguity and Perceived Organizational Characteristics Between Superintendents and Principals." Paper presented at the annual meeting of the American Education Research Association, March 21, 1982, in New York.

Callahan, Raymond E. 1975. "The American Board of Education, 1789–1960." In *Understanding School Boards*, edited by Peter J. Cistone. Lexington, Mass.: Lexington Books.

Carlson, Richard O. 1972. *School Superintendents: Careers and Performance*. Columbus, Ohio: Charles E. Merrill.

———. 1962. *Executive Succession and Organizational Change: Place-Bound and Career-Bound Superintendents of Schools*. Chicago: Midwest Administration Center, The University of Chicago.

Chesler, Mark A., et al. 1980. "Using Institutional Conflict to Achieve Change in Schools." In *Schools, Conflict, and Change*, edited by Mike M. Milstein. New York: Teachers College Press.

Cistone, Peter. 1975. "The Recruitment and Socialization of Board Members." In *Understanding School Boards*, edited by Cistone. Lexington, Mass.: Lexington Books.

Cistone, Peter J., and Iannaccone, Lawrence. 1980. "Educational Governance: Contradictions and Tendencies." *Education and Urban Society* 4: 466–85.

Clark, Burton R. 1966. "Organizational Adaptation to Professionals." In *Professionalization*, edited by Howard M. Vollmer and Donald L. Mills. Englewood Cliffs, N.J.: Prentice-Hall.

———. 1964. "Sociology of Education." In *Handbook of Modern Sociology*, edited by Robert E. L. Faris. Chicago: Rand McNally.

Cobb, Roger W., and Elder, Charles D. 1972. *Participation in American Politics: The Dynamics of Agenda Building*. Boston: Allyn and Bacon.

Coleman, James S. 1966. *Equality of Educational Opportunity.* Washington, D.C.: Government Printing Office.

———. 1963. "Comment on the Concept of Influence." *Public Opinion Quarterly* 27 (Spring): 63–82.

———. 1957. *Community Conflict.* New Jersey: The Free Press.

Colton, David, and Frelich, Allan. 1979. "Enrollment Decline and School Closings in a Large City." *Education and Urban Society* 11 (May): 396–417.

Corwin, Ronald G. 1966. *Staff Conflict in the Public Schools.* U.S. Department of Health, Education, and Welfare.

Coser, Lewis. 1961. "The Termination of Conflict." *Journal of Conflict Resolution* 5: 347–53.

———. 1956. *The Functions of Social Conflict.* Glencoe, Ill.: The Free Press.

Crain, Robert L. 1968. *The Politics of School Desegregation.* Chicago: Aldine Publishing Company.

Criswell, Larry W., and Mitchell, Douglas E. 1980. "Episodic Instability in School District Elections." *Urban Education* 2: 189–213.

Cronin, Joseph M. 1980. "Big City School Bankruptcy." Policy paper no. 80–c3. Institute for Research on Educational Finance and Governance, Stanford University, October 1980.

———. 1971. *The Control of Urban Schools.* New York: The Free Press.

Cubberley, Ellwood P. 1916. *Public School Administration.* Boston: Houghton Mifflin.

Dahl, Robert A. 1981. *Democracy in the United States.* Boston: Houghton Mifflin.

Dahl, Robert A., and Lindblom, Charles E. 1953. *Politics, Economics, and Welfare.* New York: Harper & Row.

Dahrendorf, Ralf. 1959. *Class and Class Conflict in Industrial Society.* Stanford: Stanford University Press.

Davidoff, Paul. 1965. "Advocacy and Pluralism in Planning." *Journal of American Institute of Planners* 31 (December): 331–38.

Dewey, John. 1954. *The Public and Its Problems.* Denver: The Swallow Press.

Dickinson, W. E. 1973. "The Challenges Can Be Met." In *Meeting the Challenge of School Board Leadership*, edited by National School Boards Association. Evanston: National School Boards Association.

Dodd, Lawrence C., and Schott, Richard L. 1979. *Congress and the Administrative State*. New York: John Wiley.

Donaldson, William V. 1973. "Continuing Education for City Managers." *Public Administration Review* 33 (November/December): 504ff.

Downs, Anthony. 1967. *Inside Bureaucracy*. Boston: Little, Brown.

Duckworth, Kenneth. 1981. "Creating Conditions for Effective Teaching: Implications for Educational Administration." Presentation given at the annual meeting of the National Conference of Professors of Educational Administration, August 1981 in Seattle, Washington.

Duea, Jerry, and Bishop, Walter L. 1980. "Important Differences in Public and Professional Perceptions of the Schools." *Phi Delta Kappan* (September): 50.

Dye, Thomas R. 1973. *Politics in States and Communities*. Englewood Cliffs, N.J.: Prentice-Hall.

———. 1969. *Politics in States and Communities*. Englewood Cliffs, N.J.: Prentice-Hall.

Dye, Thomas R., and Hawkins, Brett W., eds. 1967. *Politics in the Metropolis*. Columbus, Ohio: Charles E. Merrill.

Dye, Thomas R., and Zeigler, Harmon. 1984. *The Irony of Democracy*. Monterey, Calif.: Brooks-Cole.

Easton, David. 1953. *The Political System*. New York: Alfred A. Knopf.

Edelman, Murray. 1964. *The Symbolic Uses of Politics*. Urbana: University of Illinois Press.

Editorial Projects in Education. 1982. *The American Education Deskbook: 1982–83*. Washington, D.C.: Editorial Projects in Education.

Eisenberger, Katherine. 1978. "How to Learn to Manage Decline in Your School System." *The American School Board Journal* (July): 36–38.

Eisinger, Peter K. 1972. "The Pattern of Citizen Contacts with Urban Officials." In *People and Politics in Urban Society*, edited by Harlan Hahn. Beverly Hills, Calif.: Sage.

Elam, Stanley M., and Gough, Pauline B. 1980. "Comparing Lay and Professional Opinion on Gallup Poll Questions." *Phi Delta Kappan* (September): 48.

Elmore, Richard. 1981. Comments made during a seminar of the Division of Educational Policy and Management, University of Oregon.

Elmore, Richard, and McLaughlin, M. W. 1982. *Reform and Retrenchment: The Politics of California School Finance Reform*. Cambridge, Mass.: Ballinger.

Encarnation, Dennis J. 1982. "Public Support, Public Education: The Dilemma for Nonpublic Schools." *Policy Perspectives*. Stanford University: Institute for Research on Educational Finance and Governance (Winter).

Enochs, James C. 1981. "Up from Management." *Phi Delta Kappan* (November): 175–78.

Erickson, Donald A. 1972. "Moral Dilemmas of Administrative Powerlessness." *Administrator's Notebook* 20: 3–4.

Etzioni, Amatai. 1964. *Modern Organizations*. Englewood Cliffs, N.J.: Prentice-Hall.

Eulau, Heinz, and Prewitt, Kenneth. 1973. *Labyrinths of Democracy*. Indianapolis, Ind.: Bobbs-Merrill.

Eyestone, Robert. 1971. *The Threads of Public Policy: A Study in Policy Leadership*. Indianapolis, Ind.: Bobbs-Merrill.

Ficklen, Ellen. 1983. "Do You Covet a Killer Job?" *Executive Educator* (February): 17–19.

Fink, Clinton F. 1968. "Some Conceptual Difficulties in the Theory of Social Conflicts." *Journal of Conflict Resolution* 12: 412–60.

Firestone, William A. 1981. "Is 'Who Governs?' the Right Question?" *American Journal of Education* (February): 212–22.

Folwer, Charles W. 1977. "When Superintendents Fall." *American School Board Journal* (February): 2.

Fortkamp, Frank. *The Case Against Government Schools*. Cato Institute, N.D.

Freeman, John, and Hannan, Michael T. 1981. "Effects of Resources and Enrollments on Growth and Decline in School Districts." Program Report No. 81–B1. Institute for Research on Educational Finance and Governance, Stanford University, April 1981.

———. 1975. "Growth and Decline Processes in Organizations." *American Sociological Review* 40: 215–28.

Gallup, George H. 1980. "The Gallup Poll of the Public's Attitudes Toward the Public Schools." *Phi Delta Kappan* (September): 34.

Gamson, William A. 1968. *Power and Discontent*. Homewood, Ill.: Dorsey Press.

————. 1966. "Rancorous Conflict in Community Politics." *American Sociological Review* 31: 348–96.

Garms, Walter I.; Guthrie, James W.; and Pierce, Lawrence C. 1978. *School Finance: The Economics and Politics of Public Education.* Englewood Cliffs, N.J.: Prentice-Hall.

Gittell, Marilyn, et al. 1980. *Citizens Organizations: Citizen Participation in Educational Decisionmaking.* Executive Summary. Report prepared by the Institute for Responsive Education pursuant to contract Number 400–76–0115 with the National Institute of Education, May 1980.

Goertz, Margaret, and Hannigan, Janet. 1978. "Delivering a 'Thorough and Efficient' Education in New Jersey: The Impact of an Expanded Arena of Policy Making." *Journal of Education Finance* 4 (Summer): 46–64.

Golembiewski, Robert T. 1965. "Small Groups and Large Organizations." In *Handbook of Organizations*, edited by James G. March. New York: Rand-McNally.

Goodnow, Frank. 1900. *Politics and Administration.* New York: Macmillan.

Gouldner, Alvin W. 1979. *The Future of Intellectuals and the Rise of the New Class.* New York: The Seabury Press.

————. 1954. "Cosmopolitans and Locals: Toward an Analysis of Latent Social Roles." *Administrative Science Quarterly* 2: 281–306.

Greider, Calvin, et al. 1961. *Public School Administration.* New York: Ronald Press.

Griffiths, Daniel E. 1973. "Intellectualism and Professionalism." *New York University Educational Quarterly* 5 (Fall): 5–6.

Gross, Neal; Mason, Ward H.; and McEachern, Alexander W. 1958. *Explorations in Role Analysis: Studies in the School Superintendency Role.* New York: John Wiley.

Gulick, Luther and Urwick, Lyndall, eds. 1937. *Papers on the Science of Administration.* New York: Institute of Public Administration.

Guthrie, James. 1981. "Emerging Politics of Education." *Educational Evaluation and Policy Analysis* 3: 75–82.

————. 1980. "U.S. School Finance Policy 1955–1980." In *School Finance Policies and Practices: The 1980's*, edited by J. W. Guthrie. Cambridge, Mass.: Ballinger.

————. 1975. "The Erosion of Lay Control." In *Public Testimony on Public Schools*, edited by National Committee for Citizens in Education. Berkeley, Calif.: McCutchan.

————. 1954. "Public Control of Public Schools: Can We Get It Back?" *Public Affairs Report* (June): 3.

Hall, John, and Piele, Philip. 1976. "Selected Determinants of Precinct Voting Decisions in School Budget Elections." *Western Political Quarterly* 5 (September): 440–56.

Hall, Richard. 1968. "Professionalism and Bureaucratization." *American Sociological Review* 33: 92–104.

Halperin, Samuel. 1979. "The Future of Educational Governance." Prepared for the Summer Institute of the Council of Chief State School Officers, Jeffersonville, Vermont, July 1979.

Havinghurst, Robert H. 1977. "Educational Policy for Large Cities." In *Policy Studies Annual Review,* edited by Stuart Nagel. Beverly Hills, Calif.: Sage.

Henerson, Marlene E.; Morris, Lynn L.; and Fitz-Gibbons, Carol T. 1978. *How to Measure Attitudes.* Beverly Hills, Calif.: Sage.

Hill, Paul. 1979a. "Do Federal Programs Interfere with One Another?" Santa Monica, Calif.: Rand.

————. 1979b. *Enforcement and Informal Pressure on the Management of Federal Categorical Programs in Education.* Santa Monica, Calif.: Rand.

Huntington, Samuel. 1970. "Social and Institutional Dynamics of One Party Systems." In *Authoritarian Politics in Modern Society,* edited by Samuel Huntington and Clement Moore. New York: Basic Books.

Hurwitz, Mark W. 1974. "Can Local Lay School Boards Survive Much Longer with Any Real Power?" *American School Board Journal* 1: 55–57.

Iannaccone, Lawrence. 1982. "Turning-Point Election Periods in the Politics of Education." In *The Changing Politics of School Finance,* edited by Nelda H. Cambron-McCabe and Allen Odden. Cambridge, Mass.: Ballinger.

————. 1964. "The Management of Decline." *Education and Urban Society* 11: 418–30.

Iannaccone, Lawrence, and Lutz, Frank. 1970. *Politics, Power, and Policy: The Governing of Local School Districts.* Columbus, Ohio: Charles E. Merrill.

Jenks, Christopher, et al. 1972. *Inequality.* New York: Basic Books.

Jennings, Kent, and Zeigler, Harmon. 1974. *Governing American Schools*. North Scituate, Mass.: Duxbury Press.

Johnson, Chalmers. 1981. "Introduction—The Taiwan Model." In James C. Hsiung, *The Taiwan Experience*. New York: The American Association of Chinese Studies.

Johnson, Susan M. 1982. Comments at a Conference on the Effects of Collective Bargaining on School Administrative Leadership at the Center for Educational Policy and Management, University of Oregon, Eugene, Oregon.

———. 1980. "Performance-Based Layoffs in the Public Schools." *Harvard Educational Review* 50 (May): 214–33.

Just, Anne E. 1980. "Urban School Board Elections." *Education and Urban Society* 4: 421–35.

Kammerer, Galdys M. 1964. "Role Diversity of City Managers." *Administrative Science Quarterly* 8: 421–42.

Katz, Daniel; Gutek, Barbara A.; Kahn, Robert L.; and Barton, Eugenia. 1975. *Bureaucratic Encounters: A Pilot in the Evaluation of Government Services*. Ann Arbor: University of Michigan.

Key, V. O., Jr. 1961. *Public Opinion and American Democracy*. New York: Alfred A. Knopf.

Kirst, Michael. 1976. *Governance of Elementary and Secondary Education*. Aspen Institute Occasional Paper: 43.

Kirst, Michael W., and Garms, Walter I. 1980. "The Political Environment of School Finance Policy in the 1980s." In *School Finance Policies and Practices—The 1980s: A Decade of Conflict*, edited by James Guthrie. Cambridge, Mass.: Ballinger.

Kirst, Michael W., and Somers, Stephen A. 1980. "Collective Action Among California Educational Interest Groups: A Logical Response to Proposition 13." IFG School of Education, Stanford University, November 1980.

Knapp, Michael, et al. 1983. "Cumulative Effects of Federal Education Policies on Schools and Districts." SRI International, January 1983.

Kriesberg, Louis. 1973. *The Sociology of Social Conflicts*. Englewood Cliffs, New Jersey: Prentice-Hall.

Levin, Elizabeth. 1977. "Current Trends in School Finance Reform Litigation: A Commentary." *Duke Law Journal* 6: 1099–1137.

Levin, Henry M. 1983. "Commentary: Reawakening the Vigor of Urban Schools." *Education Week* (May 18): 24.

————. 1981. "Categorical Grants in Education: Rethinking the Federal Role." *Policy Perspectives*. Stanford University: Institute for Research on Educational Finance and Governance (IFG), Spring.

Lineberry, Robert L. and Sharkansky, Ira. 1971. *Urban Politics and Public Policy*. New York: Harper & Row.

Lipset, Seymour Martin, and Schwartz, Mildred A. 1966. "The Politics of Professionals." In *Professionalization*, edited by Howard J. Vollmer and Donald L. Mills. Englewood Cliffs, N.J.: Prentice-Hall.

Lipsky, Michael. 1970. *Protest in City Politics*. Chicago: Rand-McNally.

Loveridge, Robert O. 1971. *City Managers in Legislative Perspective*. Indianapolis, Ind.: Bobbs-Merrill.

Luttbeg, Normal, ed. 1974. *Public Opinion and Public Policy: Models of Political Linkages*. Homewood, Ill.: The Dorsey Press.

Lutz, Frank W. 1980. "Local School Board Decisionmaking: A Political-Anthropological Analysis." *Education and Urban Society* 4: 452–65.

Lutz, Frank, and Iannaccone, Lawrence, eds. 1978. *Public Participation in Local School Districts: The Dissatisfaction Theory of Democracy*. Lexington, Mass.: Lexington Books.

Maeroff, Gene I. 1975. "Harried School Leaders See Their Role Waning." *New York Times*, March 9, 1975, pp. 1, 29.

Majone, Giandomenico, and Wildavsky, Aaron. 1973. "Implementation as Evolution." In *Implementation*, edited by Jeffrey Pressman and Aaron Wildavsky, pp. 177–94. Berkeley: University of California Press.

March, James G., and Simon, Herbert. 1964. *Organizations*. New York: John Wiley.

————. 1957. *Organizations*. New York: John Wiley.

Marek, J. 1966. "Conflict: A Battle of Strategies." In *Operational Research and the Social Sciences*, edited by J. R. Lawrence. New York: Tavistock.

Martin, Roscoe. 1967. *Government and the Surburban School*. Syracuse: Syracuse University Press.

Masotti, Louis H. 1968. "Political Integration in Suburban Education

Communities." In *The New Urbanization*, edited by S. Greer et al. New York: St. Martin's Press.

McCarty, Donald J., and Ramsey, Charles E. 1971. *The School Managers*. Westport, Conn.: Greenwood.

McDonnell, Lorraine M., and Pascal, Anthony H. 1978. "Organized Teachers and Local Schools." In *Government in the Classroom*, edited by Mary Frase Williams. Proceedings of the Academy of Political Science N.Y., 1978.

McNeil, Elton B., ed. 1965. *The Nature of Human Conflict*. Englewood Cliffs, N.J.: Prentice-Hall.

Mintzberg, Henry. 1973. *The Nature of Managerial Work*. New York: Harper & Row.

Mitchell, Douglas E. 1980. "The Ideological Factor in School Politics." *Education and Urban Society* 4: 436–51.

Moore, Mary T. 1980a. Review of *The Politics of Educational Governance* by Harvey Tucker and Harmon Zeigler. In *The Politics of Education Bulletin* 9 (Winter): 14.

———. 1980b. Review of *Professionals versus the Public* by Harvey Tucker and Harmon Zeigler. In *The Politics of Education Bulletin* 9 (Winter).

Moore, Mary T., et al. 1983. "The Interaction of Federal and Related State Education Programs: Executive Summary." Washington, D.C.: Educational Policy Research Institute, February 1983.

Morris, V.; Crowson, R.; Hurwitz, E., Jr.; Porter-Gehrie, C. 1981. *The Urban Principal: Discretionary Decision-Making in a Large Educational Organization*. Research Report. University of Illinois at Chicago Circle (March 1981).

Morstein-Marx, Fritz, ed. 1946. *Elements of Public Administration*. Englewood Cliffs, N.J.: Prentice-Hall.

Mosher, Frederick C. 1982. *Democracy and the Public Service*. New York: Oxford University Press.

Murnane, Richard J. 1981. "Seniority Rules and Educational Productivity: Understanding the Consequences of a Mandate for Equality." *American Journal of Education* 90 (November): 14–38.

Murphy, Jerome T. 1982. "Progress and Problems: The Paradox of State Reform." In *Policy Making in Education*, edited by Ann Liebermen and Milbrey W. McLaughlin. *The Eighty-first Yearbook of the National Society for the Study of Education*, vol. 1.

National Commission on Excellence in Education. 1983. *A Nation at Risk: The Imperative for Educational Reform.* A Report to the Nation and the Secretary of Education. Washington, D.C.: U.S. Government Printing Office.

National Institute of Education Planning Unit. 1972. *Program Planning Notes from the Interim Report of NIE*, pp. 10–11.

National School Boards Association. 1975. *Survey of Public Education in the Nation's Big City Schools.* Evanston, Ill.: National School Board Association.

———. *Survey of Public Education.*

Nebgen, Mary K. 1978. "Conflict Management in Schools." *Administrator's Notebook* 26: 1–4, 77–78.

New York Times. 1983. "Electing Board for City Schools Has Political Air." March 15, p. 84.

Olson, Mancur. 1982. *The Rise and Decline of Nations.* New Haven: Yale University Press.

Orfield, Gary. 1969. *The Reconstruction of Southern Education: The Schools and the 1964 Civil Rights Act.* New York: John Wiley.

Page, Richard S. 1971. "The Ideological-Philosophical Setting of American Public Administration." In *Public Administration in a Time of Turbulence*, edited by Dwight Waldo. Scranton, Penn.: Chandler.

Peterson, Paul E. 1976. *School Politics Chicago Style.* Chicago, Ill.: University of Chicago Press.

———. 1974. "The Politics of American Education." In *Review of Research in Education*, edited by F. W. Kerlinger and J. B. Carroll. Itasca, Ill.: F. E. Peacock.

Pierce, Lawrence. 1975. "Teachers' Organizations and Bargaining: Power Imbalance in the Public Sphere." In *Public Testimony on Public Schools*, edited by National Committee for Citizens in Education, Commission on Educational Governance. Berkeley, Calif.: McCutchan.

Piven, Frances Fox, and Cloward, Richard A. 1977. *Poor People's Movements.* New York: Pantheon.

Radin, Beryl A. 1978. "Equal Educational Opportunity and Federalism." In *Government in the Classroom: Dollars and Power in Education*, edited by Mary Frase Williams. New York: Academy of Political Science.

Ranney, Austin. 1966. *The Governing of Men*. New York: Holt, Rinehart, and Winston.

Reisman, Jane. 1982. "Conflict Management in Public Bureaucracies: The Case of School Superintendents and City Managers." Ph.D. dissertation, University of Oregon.

Rogow, Arnold A., and Lasswell, Harold D. 1963. *Power, Corruption, and Rectitude*. Englewood Cliffs, N.J.: Prentice-Hall.

Roizen, Judy; Fulton, Oliver; and Trow, Martin. 1978. "Technical Report: 1975 Carnegie Council National Surveys of Higher Education." Berkeley, Calif.: Center for Studies in Higher Education, University of California.

Rosenthal, Alan. 1969. *Pedagogues and Power*. Syracuse: Syracuse University Press.

Ross, E. A. 1930. *Principles of Sociology*. New York: Century.

Rost, Joseph C. 1982. "The Politics of Leadership." Paper presented at the annual meeting of the American Educational Research Conference, March 21, 1982, in New York.

Rudensky, Maria. 1982. "A Primer on PACs." *The School Administrator* (September): 16–17.

Salisbury, Robert H. 1980. *Citizen Participation in the Public Schools*. Lexington, Mass.: Lexington Books.

Schattschneider, E. E. 1960. *The Semi-Sovereign People*. New York: Holt.

Schlesinger, Joseph. 1966. *Ambition and Politics*. Chicago: Rand McNally.

Schmidt, Stuart M., and Kochan, Thomas A. 1972. "Conflict: Toward Conceptual Clarity." *Administrative Science Quarterly* 17: 359–70.

Schmuck, Richard A., et al. 1975. *Consultation for Innovative Schools*. Eugene, Oregon: Center for Educational Policy and Management, University of Oregon.

Schulman, Mark A. 1979. "The Impact of Three Mile Island." *Public Opinion* (June/July): 7–9. See also ibid., p. 26.

Schultze, William A. 1974. *Urban and Community Politics*. North Scituate, Mass.: Duxbury Press.

Schumpeter, Joseph A. 1942. *Capitalism, Socialism, and Democracy*. New York: Harper & Row.

Scott, Richard W. 1966. "Professionals in Bureaucracies—Areas of Conflict." In *Professionalism*, edited by Howard Vollmer and Donald L.
Mills. Englewood Cliffs, N.J.: Prentice-Hall.

Seiler, J. A. 1963. "Diagnosing Interdepartmental Conflict." *Harvard
Business Review* 41: 121–32.

Serrano vs. Priest. 1971. 96 Cal, Reptr (1971).

Sherman, Joel D. 1982. *Prospects for Financing Elementary/Secondary Education in the States: Congressionally Mandated Study of School Finance*.
Final Report, vol. 1. Report to Congress from the Secretary of Education, December 1982.

Simmel, George. 1955. *Conflict and the Web of Group Affiliations*. Glencoe,
Ill.: Free Press.

Simon, Herbert. 1947. *Administrative Behavior*. New York: The Free
Press.

Simons, Janet M., and Dwyer, Barbara. 1978. "Education of the Handicapped." In *Government in the Classroom: Dollars and Power in Education*, edited by Mary Frase Williams. New York: Academy of Political
Science.

Sorokin, Pitrim A. 1927. *Social Mobility*. New York: Harper & Row.

Steele, Donald J.; Working, Russell J., and Biernacki, L. 1981. "Care and
Feeding of Interest Groups: Interest Groups as Seen by a City School
Superintendent." *Education and Urban Society*, 13 (February):
257–70.

Stelzer, Leigh. 1975. "Institutionalizing Conflict Response: The Case of
School Boards." In *The Policy of the School: New Research in Educational Politics*, edited by Frederick Wirt. Lexington, Mass.: Lexington Books.

Stillman, Richard J., II. 1974. "Public Professionalism in Perspective: City
Managers, Career Diplomats, School Superintendents Compared
and Contrasted." In *Rise of the City Manager: A Public Professional
in Local Government*, edited by Richard Stillman. Albuquerque: University of New Mexico Press.

————. 1973. "Woodrow Wilson and the Study of Administration: A New
Look at an Old Essay." *American Political Science Review* 67 (June):
582–88.

Teitlebaum, Herbert, and Hiller, Richard. 1977. "Bilingual Education: The
Legal Mandate." *Harvard Educational Review* 47: 138–70.

Thomas, Kenneth W., and Kilmann, Ralph H. 1974. *Conflict Mode Instrument*. Tuxedo, New York: Xicom.

Thompson, John Thomas. 1976. *Policymaking in American Education*. Englewood Cliffs, N.J.: Prentice-Hall.

Torgovnik, Efraim. 1969. *Determinants in Managerial Selection*. Washington, D.C.: International City Management Association.

Truman, David. 1951. *The Governmental Process*. New York: Alfred A. Knopf.

Tucker, Harvey J., and Zeigler, Harmon. 1980. *Professionals versus the Public: Attitudes, Communication, and Response in Local School Districts*. New York: Longman.

————. 1978. *The Quest for Responsive Government: An Essay on State and Local Politics*. North Scituate, Mass.: Duxbury Press.

Tyack, David. 1974. *The One Best System*. Cambridge, Mass.: Harvard University Press.

Underwood, Kenneth E.; Fortune, James C.; and Dodge, Harold W. 1982. "Here's How You Would Chop Your Budget." *The American School Board Journal* 1: 21, 24–25.

U.S. Bureau of the Census. 1979. "Small Area Data Notes." Washington, D.C.: U.S. Government Printing Office.

Van Geel, Tyl. 1976. *Authority to Control the School Program*. Lexington, Mass.: D. C. Heath.

Walker, Jack L. 1971. "Innovation in State Politics." In *Politics in the American States*, edited by Herbert Jacob and Kenneth N. Vines. Boston: Little, Brown.

Weatherley, Richard; Narver, Betty Jane; and Elmore, Richard. 1981. "School Closures in Seattle: The Politics and Management of Decline." Unpublished paper. Seattle, Wash.: University of Washington.

Wilensky, Harold L. 1967. *Organizational Intelligence*. New York: Basic Books.

Wilson, James Q. 1976. "Social Science: The Public Disenchantment, A Symposium." *The American Scholar* (Summer): 358.

Wilson, James Q., and Banfield, Edward C. 1964. "Public Regardingness as a Value Premise in Voting Behavior." *American Political Science Review* 58 (December): 876–77.

Wirt, Frederick. 1977. "School Policy Culture and State Decentralization." In *The Politics of Education*, edited by Jay Scribner. 1977 Yearbook of the National Society for the Study of Education.

Wirt, Frederick, and Christovich, Leslie. 1982. "Are Superintendents Paper Tigers?" *School Administrator* (September): 12–13.

Wirt, Frederick, and Kirst, Michael. 1972. *The Political Web of American Schools*. Boston: Little, Brown.

Wolcott, Harry F. 1977. *Teachers vs. Technocrats*. Eugene, Oregon: Center for Educational Policy and Management, University of Oregon.

Yates, Douglas. 1982. *Bureaucratic Democracy*. Cambridge, Mass.: Harvard University Press.

Yeager, Robert F. 1979. "Rationality and Retrenchment: The Use of a Computer Simulation to Aid Decision Making in School Closings." *Education and Urban Society* 11 (May): 296–312.

Zald, Mayer. 1969. "The Power and Functions of Boards of Directors: A Theoretical Synthesis." *American Journal of Sociology* 75 (July): 97–101.

Zeigler, Harmon; Tucker, Harvey J.; and Wilson, L. A., II. 1977. "How School Control was Wrested from the People." *Phi Delta Kappan* (March): 534–39.

Zeigler, Harmon; Jennings, M. Kent; and Peak, G. Wayne. 1974. *Governing American Schools: Political Interaction in Local School Districts*. North Scituate, Mass.: Duxbury Press.

Zeigler, Harmon, and Peak, Wayne. 1977. *Interest Groups in American Society*, 2nd ed. Englewood Cliffs, N.J.: Prentice-Hall, 1972.

INDEX

INDEX

About the Authors

Harmon Zeigler has published widely in the fields of political science and education. Among his best known works are *Interest Groups in American Society* (Prentice-Hall, 1964; 2nd edition, 1972); *The Political Life of American Teachers* (Prentice-Hall, 1967); *The Irony of Democracy* (with Thomas R. Dye, Brooks/Cole, 6th edition, 1984); *Governing American Schools* (with Kent Jennings, Duxbury, 1974); *Professionals Versus the Public: Attitudes, Communication, and Response in Local School Districts* (with Harvey J. Tucker, Longman, 1980); and *American Politics in the Media Age* (with Thomas R. Dye, Brooks/Cole, 1983).

Ellen Kehoe, D. Ed., University of Rochester, 1981. Research Associate, Center for Educational Policy and Management, University of Oregon, 1979–82. Assistant Professor of Educational Administration, Teachers College, Columbia University.

Jane Reisman, Ph.D., University of Oregon, 1982. Research Specialist and Lecturer, the Ohio State University, 1983–84. Assistant Professor of Sociology, Pacific Lutheran University, Tacoma, Washington.